THE LAST
TSAR

Design : Margueritte Shenguelija
Lydia Upit
Translated from the Russian by Vladimir Pavlov

Design by A.L. Semyonov
Special photographs by V.N. Kornyushin
Editor: Margueritte Shenguelija
Art Director: Natasha Trofimova
Editorial Director : Paul André
Production: Presse +

Jacket: Nicolas II taking part in a religious procession
in the Kremlin. Moscow, 1913

Printed by Mariogros, Turin (Italy)
for Parkstone Press
Copyright 1st term 1996
ISBN 1-85995-208-9

LARISSA YERMILOVA

THE LAST TSAR

PARKSTONE
PLANETA

January, 1613. A deputation of boyars and high-ranking clergy followed by a crowd is marching along the ancient road from Kostroma to the Ipatiev Monastery, carrying a miracle-working ikon of Our Lady, the Gospels, a cross, the royal staff and a huge mica lantern. The deputation's task is to advise the young boyar Mikhail Romanov, who is living with his nun-mother Marfa at the Ipatiev Monastery, of the decision of the Zemsky Sobor (the Grand National Assembly) to elect him to tsardom. They are going to ask Mikhail Fyodorovich Romanov to accept the trust put in him by the Russian people.

This event was preceded by a long period of bloody strife in Russia which came to be known as the «Times of Troubles», during which the Russian state practically disintegrated and the country was reduced to ruin and chaos. During the «Times of Troubles» Russia was occupied by Poland, Novgorod and Pskov were seized by Sweden, Russian lands were ransacked by Lithuanians and Poles and by huge bands of brigands. For a while a usurper - the False Dmitry - ruled in Moscow, installed on the Russian throne by the Polish army. It seemed the country was totally lost. But at that critical moment the Russian people, inspired by patriotic feelings, rallied against the invaders.

From the porch of the Cathedral of the Assumption in Nizhni Novgorod Kuzma Minin appealed to the people to rise to the defence of their country. A volunteer army was formed and led by Prince Pozharsky to liberate Moscow. Russia won a chance to restore its unity and statehood.

Immediately upon the liberation of Moscow the higher clergy and elected representatives were summoned to Moscow for an assembly, the purpose of which was to choose a tsar. According to the historian Vassily Klyuchevsky, this was «the first ever truly representative Zemsky Sobor, in which even the common folk of town and country took part.» The deputies spent three days fasting, to purify themselves of the sins of the «Times of Troubles», and praying that God should direct them to elect a tsar «not of their inclination» but by the will of the people, sanctified by religion. Petitions were received by the Sobor from the gentry and the merchant class, from the cities of the Russian North and even from the Cossacks in the South - all pleading the cause of the young boyar Mikhail Romanov. The chronicles say on the subject: «The superiors and all people, praying for God's mercy, began to think how to make a righteous choice for the Muscovy throne, given of God and not of Man... And the same thought came to all, not only to the lords and the civil servants, but also to all common Orthodox Christians... And they cried of one accord: by the love of us all, we shall have as sovereign of the Moscow state Mikhail Fyodorovich Romanov Yuriev». The final decision was left to the Russian people. And word came from everywhere: «All people, young and old, have the same thought: Mikhail Fyodorovich Romanov should be Tsar». It was widely known that Mikhail's father, the Metropolitan Philaret, when besieged by the Poles in the city of Rostov, locked himself in the cathedral with the townsfolk and urged them to fight to the last and not surrender. The enemy finally broke into the cathedral, massacred its defenders and took the Metropolitan prisoner. Another weighty factor for the sixteen-year-old Mikhail was his connection with the lawful royal dynasty. He was the grandson of Ivan the Terrible.

And so, on January 13, 1613, the deputation appealed to the young boyar at the Ipatiev Monastery to accept the sceptre of the Tsar of Russia.

To begin with, his mother Marfa was adamant in refusing. But eventually she knelt before the miracle-working ikon of Our Lady and blessed Mikhail to tsardom.

Patriarch Philaret, father of Michael (Mikhail Fyodorovich) Romanov, Fyodor Nikitich Romanov in the world. Drawing.

The first thing the young Tsar did after being annointed to sovereignty, was to obtain the release of his father from imprisonment and to make him the Metropolitan of Moscow and all Russia. The return of Metropolitan Philaret was an event of outstanding importance. In Moscow's Cathedral of the Assumption he was consecrated Patriarch and, until his death, not only headed the church but was also associated with his son in the government of the country on an equal footing.

A new form of government was established at the beginning of Tsar Mikhail's reign. This was effected by the Zemsky Sobor, which was convened from elected representatives from all over Russia. During the reign of Tsar Mikhail this assembly worked in close collaboration with the royal power and did a lot to foster patriotic feelings in the country.

Patriarch Philaret was largely responsible for the successes scored by Russia in internal and external policies under Tsar Mikhail. The chronicle reports: «A peace was concluded with the Poles, and also with Sweden, who agreed to return Novgorod and Ladoga; an earth rampart was built to defend the borders of Russia from raids launched from the Crimean Steppe, and towns were built along it. In 1637, the Don Cossacks captured Azov, a delegation was sent for the first time to China, peace was established with the Turks and the Persians, and embassies exchanged... The devastated Moscow was restored and improved.»

Tsar Mikhail ruled for 32 years, and died on July 13, 1645, at the age of forty-nine. He was interred in the Archangel Cathedral in Moscow.

Immediately after his demise, on the morning of July 13, 1645, Moscow pledged allegiance to his son Alexei Mikhailovich (he was to rule until 1676). The young man accepted tsardom with his father's blessing. The coronation was celebrated with great splendour.

Alexei Mikhailovich, the «meek tsar», was a well educated man who had a good knowledge of the church and lay literature of his time. He also possessed a literary gift. His letters and decrees were written in lively imaginative language. His extensive reading of ecclesiastical writings caused him to develop a profound piousness. The Tsar prayed a lot, observed fasts and knew all the church statutes by heart. Yet it was his reign that witnessed a schism in the Orthodox Church and a conflict between the Tsar and the Patriarch. These developments in the religious life of the

Election of Tsar Mikhail Fyodorovich Romanov. Drawing.

*Tsar Mikhail Fyodorovich.
Drawing.*

country marked an important change in the relationship between Church and State.

A view began to spread in Russian ecclesiastical circles and in the royal palace itself that amendments needed to be introduced into the Russian liturgical books and rituals to correct errors which had crept into them in the early years of Christianity in Russia, and to make them conform to the Greek practices.

The work of correcting the liturgy and introducing other necessary reforms was undertaken by Patriarch Nikon with the approval of the Tsar. But his reforms met with violent opposition on the part of the lower clergy and the common people, who regarded these changes as the loss of national traditions and heretical concessions to the Catholics and Lutherans. Many were adamant in resisting the innovations and remained true to the old Russian religious practices. The most fanatical of the upholders of the «Old Faith» was arch-priest Avvakum, who suffered sorely for his convictions. Questions of faith became burning issues in the life of Russia.

Persecution of the opponents of reform was launched; the most intractable of them, such as Boyarina Morozova and Princess Urusova, were tortured and confined to prison. The monk Avraamy was executed in Moscow, the uprising in the Solovetsky Monastery was ruthlessly put down. Arch-priest Avvakum was burnt alive. The Old Believers retaliated to these reprisals by mass self-immolation.

Patriarch Nikon insisted that the spiritual power was superior to the temporal one and that the Patriarch was subject to no earthly authority. He also denied the divine right of kings. The Tsar's patience exhausted, he broke with Nikon, and the Church Assembly held in 1666-1667 deposed the Patriarch, who had become notorious as the persecutor of «ancient piety». Nikon was exiled to a monastery. The authority of the Patriarch was thus undermined, and the ground was prepared for the abolition of the patriarchate in Russia, which was brought about by Alexei Mikhailovich's son Peter the Great. The Old Believers opposed this annexation of the power of church administration by the tsar. They formed communities in which they lived according to the old religious precepts.

Under Tsar Alexei Mikhailovich Russia laid claim to Western and Southern Russian territories. In the mid-17th century, Muscovy advocated the

Election of Tsar Mikhail Fyodorovich. Icon.

Wonder-working icon of the Holy Virgin of St.Theodore Ipatievsky.

unification of all Slav lands under the Russian crown. In 1649, the Ukrainian Hetman Bogdan Khmelnitsky started negotiations for the «acceptance of Little Russia under Moscow's protection», the Ukrainians having blood and religious kinship with the Russian people. In 1653, the Zemsky Sobor in Moscow took the relevant decision. But to implement it, Russia had to wage a war against Poland for possession of the Ukraine. At the same time, it had to fight Sweden over the Baltic lands. Of course, Russia could not hope to win two wars at once and, in the end, had to cede Lithuania and Byelorussia to Poland and relinquish its claims to the Baltic seaboard. The lands of Novgorod and Pskov also remained under Sweden. A compromise solution was reached as regards the Ukraine. The right bank of the Dnieper (Western Ukraine) remained subject to Poland, while Eastern Ukraine, on the left bank of the Dnieper, with the capital city of Kiev, was reunited with Russia.

Here is what a chronicler wrote about the tempestuous internal and external events that befell Russia during the reign of Tsar Alexei Mikhailovich, «During his reign, the Don Cossack Stenka Razin went on a rampage on the Volga and in the Caspian Sea. He seized Astrakhan and other cities and laid them waste. He burnt down the sea-going ships, which had been built in Astrakhan, including the largest of them named 'Orel'. In the end he was captured and incarcerated in Moscow. Twice the Crimean Khan raided Russia, but if he won victory during the first campaign, in the second summer the Crimeans were completely routed.»

Tsar Alexei Mikhailovich set up linen- and silk-weaving factories, encouraged trade, rebuilt churches and monasteries and enlarged and adorned Moscow.

The reign of the «meek tsar» lasted for 30 years and 5 months. He died on January 29, 1676, and was interred at the Archangel Cathedral in Moscow. He had two sons from his first marriage, to Maria Miloslavsky, - Fyodor and Ivan, and one from the second, to Natalia Naryshkin. The name of this third son was Peter.

On his death-bed the Tsar appointed his elder son Fyodor to the Russian throne. The young tsar was weak in health and died six years later, in 1682. During his reign, the country was ruled by two rival families, relatives of his mother, the Miloslavskys, and relatives of his step-mother, the

Monastery. Drawing.

Tsar Fyodor Alekseyevich. Drawing.

Naryshkins. The Miloslavskys soon managed to shoulder the Naryshkins aside, and the widow of the late tsar, Natalia Naryshkin, was forced to leave the Kremlin and move with her young son Peter to the village of Preobrazhenskoye on the outskirts of Moscow.

The Miloslavsky clan was headed by Tsar Alexei's fourth daughter Sophia, a woman endowed with a shrewd mind, strong character and overpowering ambition. All of Tsar Alexei's daughters had received a western-style education under the tutelage of the monk-scholar and writer Simeon Polotsky. Sophia, his most gifted pupil, decided to usurp her father's throne. Tsar Fyodor died on April 27, 1682. This marked the beginning of Sophia's dramatic struggle for the throne. The next in the order of succession was Ivan, but he was a very sick young man. The Zemsky Sobor, convened to decide the issue, ruled in favour of the ten-year-old Peter. Then Sophia instigated the *streltsy*, the troops of the reformed army whose devotion she had worked hard to win, to revolt against the Naryshkins. Before the eyes of young Peter, the boyar Matveyev and Peter's uncles Pyotr and Afanasy Naryshkin were speared to death by the mutinous *streltsy*. The terrified Boyar Duma complied with their demands. Ivan and Peter were jointly proclaimed tsars and, during their minority, Sophia was to act as regent.

Eventually the *streltsy*, led by their general Prince Khovansky, openly declared their support for the Old Faith. This prompted Sophia to change her attitude to them and she succeeded in ensuring their non-interference in the affairs of state. During her rule she relied a great deal on her devoted favourite Prince Vassily Golitsyn. An educated man, who had a command of Latin and Polish, he planned to form a regular Russian army and to free the landed serfs. He led two abortive campaigns against the Crimean Tatars.

When Peter grew up, married Yevdokiya Lopukhina, and began thinking of taking power into his own hands, Sophia conspired with the *streltsy* to get rid of him. Fearing for his life, Peter fled from Preobrazhenskoye to the Trinity-Sergius Monastery, where he gathered a troop of devoted followers. The foreign regiment commanded by General Gordon also sided with him. Having come to an agreement with his brother Ivan on joint rule without Sophia, Peter gave orders to have Sophia incarcerated in the Novodevichy Nunnery.

Prince Pozharsky's banner.

Tsarevna Sophia. Drawing.

The personality of Peter the First amazed both his contemporaries and later generations. He appeared to the nation not in mantle and crown, but axe in hand, as a working man and a head of the household. He was a man of great energy and outstanding administrative ability, and was prepared to listen to criticism and to follow wise advice.

The activities of Tsar Peter had great consequences for the fate of Russia. The most painful setback Muscovy had suffered in the 17th century, in Tsar Peter's opinion, was the loss of the Baltic seaboard, which gave it an outlet to the west. Peter's victory over the Swedes in the Great Northern War of 1700-1721, the restitution of the Baltic lands, which had been seized by Sweden, and the establishment of a new capital, St. Petersburg, on the Gulf of Finland made the European nations aware of Russia's new strength and unity and raised her prestige among the European nations.

The impressive military victories and the expansion of the Russian borders brought about «the unification of formerly divided eastern and western halves of Europe in common activities by involving in these activities the Slav tribe, which only now began to participate in Europe's life through its representative, the Russian people.» Thus wrote the historian Sergei Solovyov. Peter I worked resolutely to raise his country to the European level. With an iron hand he carried out urgent reforms which changed the very tenor of life in the country. He formed a regular army, built a navy and set up an administrative system of education.

Sergei Solovyov assessed the results of Peter's reforms thus: «In the internal life of the country, foundations were laid for a new political and civic order. Society was aroused to political activities by the introduction of collegiate administration, the elective principle and local self-government. The oath of allegiance was now sworn not only to the tsar but also to the state, which introduced the common people to the concept of the state's importance. In private law, measures were taken to protect the individual; The Russian was freed from the fetters of the family by Peter's stress on personal achievement, a poll-tax was introduced, marriage by coercion on the part of parents or landlords was prohibited, and the woman was liberated from the prison of her home».

The common people did not appreciate the importance of Tsar Peter's reforms. Several uprisings broke out during his reign, by *streltsy* in

Battle of Poltava. Drawing.

Emperor Peter the Great. Drawing.

Moscow, *streltsy* and working men in Astrakhan, by peasants and Cossacks led by Kondrat Bulavin. All of them were cruelly suppressed. Clearly aware of the political and administrative tasks facing Russia, Tsar Peter refused to take account of the traditional mentality and morality of his people, who regarded his reforms as encroachments on popular customs and beliefs. Besides, they were sorely tried by forced labour, inflicted on them for the implementation of the Tsar's innovations. A yawning gap appeared between the upper and the lower strata of society. «Among the popular masses the reform had a very unreliable and shaky footing,» wrote the historian Vassily Klyuchevsky.

And yet Peter the Great succeeded in fundamentally restructuring all aspects of Russian life. Ivan Neplyuyev, a noted diplomat of the time, paid the following homage to the work he accomplished: «This monarch brought our country into line with the other powers, forced them to recognise us as people in our own right; in a word, wherever you look in Russia, everything can be traced back to him, and those who will work for Russia in the future will also draw on this source. Russia...has been included in the community of political nations». The outstanding Russian poet Fyodor Tyutchev summarised Tsar Peter's achievement thus: «A mammoth hand drew back the curtain, and the Europe of Charlemagne found itself facing the Europe of Peter the Great».

In his economic activities Tsar Peter was guided by the rule that for a state to grow rich it must export more and import less. To avoid impoverishment, a nation must produce everything for its consumption and not depend on others.

Peter the Great fostered various industries, confident that the capital invested in them would be repaid very soon. At the time of his death Russia had no foreign debts whatever. He was truly a thrifty manager of the country's wealth. He encouraged the rational use of forests, but severely punished those guilty of their short-sighted destruction. He was against all waste and ordered that even timber pine branches should be used to make axles.

When Peter the Great died on January 27, 1725, the whole country was plunged into mourning, feeling that Russia had lost a mighty ruler, who had her best interests at heart.

The founding of St. Petersburg in 1703. Drawing.

Peter died without leaving an heir. «A great authority and builder of his state, Peter was least informed about one little corner of it - his family, his home, where he used to be no more than a guest,» wrote Klyuchevsky. «He did not get on with his first wife (Yevdokiya Lopukhina), had cause to be displeased with his second wife, Empress Catherine Alexeyevna, and fell out completely with his son, failing to protect him from hostile influences, which proved to be the tsarevich's undoing». Tsarevich Alexei, Peter's son by the first marriage, died in a cell of the Peter and Paul Fortress after being tried for treason and sentenced to death. Peter's sons by his second marriage died in infancy.

On February 5, 1722, Peter the Great issued an edict, which cancelled the previous order of succession to the throne and instituted a new procedure: the successor was to be appointed by the reigning emperor. But he appointed no one to succeed himself. «Peter vacillated for years, trying to decide on a successor, and on the brink of death, having lost the faculty of speech, merely managed to scribble in a shaky hand: 'Give everything to...' and the weakened hand failed to write the last words legibly,» wrote Klyuchevsky.

During the night, while Peter the Great was on his death-bed, the Guards carried out the first palace coup of the many that were to follow. Instigated by the new nobility, who owed their rise to the emperor, they opted for Peter's wife Catherine. She ascended to the Russian throne as Empress Catherine I and reigned from 1725 to 1727. There was considerable opposition to this foreigner who, it was averred, had cheated the lawful heir - Peter's grandson, the son of his dead son Alexei - of his right to succession. Under Catherine I, «a weak and voluptuous woman», real power was in the hands of the Supreme Privy Council, composed of the greatest actual dignitaries of the latter years of Peter's reign. The factual ruler of the country was Peter's favourite Alexander Menshikov, who was more concerned with his own enrichment than with the country's benefit and the people's wellbeing.

Before her death in 1727, Empress Catherine I was prevailed upon to name as her successor the twelve-year-old grandson of Peter the Great, who ascended the throne as Emperor Peter II on May 7, 1727 and reigned until January 19, 1730.

Empress Catherine I. Drawing.

Empress Elizaveta Petrovna. Drawing.

This is how the historian Nikolai Kostomarov described the mood of society at that period:

«Back on October 21 (1727) a royal manifesto announced that the coronation would take place in Moscow, and all November St. Petersburg was rife with rumours. Supporters of Peter's reforms and all foreigners who lived and served in Russia, as well as diplomats who based their political plans on hopes for friendship with Russia, were extremely apprehensive; they foresaw that, once taken to the old capital, the boy-tsar would never return to St.Petersburg. The Old Believers would fuddle his young brain and would not allow him to follow the road blazed by his grandfather. Which of the two Russias would win, the new one created by Peter the Great, so to speak, or the old one? This was the question that hung in the balance. The newly built St. Petersburg was part of new Russia; Moscow, the capital of previous tsars, was bound to old Russia. If new Russia triumphed, the capital would remain in St. Petersburg; if not, Moscow would regain its former stature.

«Tsar Peter II left St. Petersburg with his court on January 9, 1728. No such journey had ever been undertaken by a Russian tsar, not counting the trip of Peter the Great to Moscow for the coronation of his wife Catherine. But now everything was done on a much grander scale. Anyone who had anything to do with the administration followed the tsar to the old capital, and St.Petersburg, as a foreign envoy remarked, suddenly became a desert.»

During the short reign of the boy-emperor the fall occurred of the mighty Menshikov, and the Princes Dolgoruky rose to eminence in his stead. Menshikov, an autocratic ruler, a man of enormous weath and extravagant habits, was stripped of all titles and property and exiled to the town of Beryozov in Siberia, where he soon died.

In early 1730 Peter II contracted smallpox, of which he died on January 19, 1730. With his death the Romanov male line of succession was cut short. The question of an heir to the throne was discussed by the Supreme Privy Council, which made an attempt to establish a constitutional monarchy. Prince Dmitry Golitsyn, an influential member of the Council and a man of European education, formulated conditions that would restrict the autocracy and nominated a candidate for the throne - the Dowager Duchess of Courland, Anne, the daughter of Ivan, Tsar Peter's brother. As it happened, it was a very unfortunate choice. Anne unhesitatingly signed the document limiting her powers and placing her under the control of the Privy Council but, once installed on the throne, made skilful use of the aristocracy's opposition to the Privy Council and, abrogating all «conditions» and «petitions», assumed unlimited autocratic power. Soon after, the Supreme Privy Council was dissolved altogether. All affairs of state were now handled by a Cabinet of three ministers.

Vassily Klyuchevsky has left us a vivid description of the reign of Empress Anne (1730-1740) and her court:

«That reign was one of the grimmest pages in our history, and the darkest spot on this page was the person of the Empress herself. Tall and stout, with a masculine rather than a feminine face, hard-hearted by nature and hardened still more by her early widowhood among diplomatic schemes and court intrigues in Courland, where she was regarded as a Russo-Prusso-Polish toy and treated accordingly, she brought to Moscow, at the age of 37, a malicious and uncultivated mind and a savage thirst for belated pleasures and crude entertainments. Having, by a pure fluke, escaped from a miserable Lithuanian hole to attain unlimited power in vast Russia, she threw herself into festivities and amusements which astonished foreign observers by their extravagant luxury and bad taste. She surrounded herself with female clowns and fools, whom she sought out practically throughout the empire. By their incessant gabbling, they chased away her corrosive feeling of loneliness and estrangement from the country she ruled, where she felt constantly threatened. Her greatest pleasure was to humiliate a person, to gloat at his abasement, to exult at his discomfiture.

«Empress Anne did not trust Russians and surrounded herself, for protection, with a crowd of foreigners whom she had recruited in Mitava and other German backwoods.

«The Cabinet was something in the nature of the Empress's personal chancellery, or else a travesty of the Privy Council. It concerned itself with important legislative matters on the one hand, and on the other provided hares for the court kitchen and checked the bills for lace purchased by the Empress. A puppet of autocratic power, deprived of legal responsibility, the Cabinet, by its meddling, only wrought havoc in government bodies and was truly a reflection of the devious mind of its creator and the very nature of that gloomy reign.

«The Secret Investigatory Chancellery, a revival of the Preobrazhensky Prikaz disbanded during the reign of Peter II, worked indefatigably to instill respect for the imperial power and assure its security through informers and torture...»

Under Empress Anne, the expansion of the navy was discontinued and the size of the army reduced. The soldiers were clad in uniforms followed the German fashion, and their training in Prussian military regulations. Major blunders were committed in the diplomatic field. The ill-judged Russo-Turkish War of 1735-1739, which involved the loss of more than a hundred thousand soldiers, brought no appreciable gains. Russia did not obtain an outlet to the Black Sea, nor even to the Azov Sea. Its southern borders remained open to the raids of Crimean Tartars.

Empress Anne named as her successor her infant grand-nephew Ivan Antonovich, the great-grandson of Tsar Ivan, Peter the Great's brother. Biron, heartily hated by all and sundry, was to be regent. Field-Marshal Minich, who hankered after power himself, arrested Biron on November 9, 1740, and Ivan Antonovich's mother Anna Leopoldovna, Empress Anne's niece, was appointed regent. But by then Russian society and the Guards were sated with the rule of foreigners and wanted to see enthroned a person who had no German leanings or connections. The Guards

Empress Catherine II. Drawing.

regiments favoured Elisabeth, the younger daughter of Peter the Great and Catherine I. On the night of November 25, 1741, Elisabeth came to the barracks of the Preobrazhensky Regiment and appealed to the Guards to proclaim her Empress.

Elisabeth reigned for 20 years (1741-1761). The infant Ivan Antonovich was confined in the Schliesselburg Fortress, where he languished in complete isolation for 23 years, until 1764, when the officer Mirovich made an attempt to liberate him, in the course of which Ivan Antonovich was killed. «Peace-loving and care-free by nature,» Vassily Klyuchevsky writes about Empress Elisabeth, «she was forced to wage wars during almost half of her reign. She won battles against the foremost strategist of that time, Frederick the Great, captured Berlin, and lost masses of soldiers in the fields of Zorndorf and Kunersdorf, yet never since the reign of Tsarevna Sophia had life in Russia been so easy, and no other reign, until 1762, left so pleasant a memory. With Western Europe exhausted by two large coalition wars, Elisabeth, with her 300,000-strong army, could have commanded European destinies.»

Foreigners were amazed by the beauty and magnificence of palaces which were built during Empress Elisabeth's reign. The most outstanding architect of that time was Bartholomew Rastrelli, who built the Smolny Cathedral in St. Petersburg and St. Andrew's Cathedral in Kiev, and who completed the construction of the Winter Palace.

Already in 1742, Empress Elisabeth made a decisive step to secure the succession to the Russian throne for her father's line. She summoned from Kiel the son of her deceased elder sister, Anna, Charles Peter Ulrich, Duke of Holstein-Gottorp, and proclaimed him heir-apparent under the Russian name of Pyotr Fyodorovich. After Elisabeth's death on December 25, 1761, he became the Russian Emperor, Peter III, but reigned for only a few months. He was physically weak, mentally infantile and emotionally undeveloped. His wife Catherine II wrote in her memoirs: «He looked like a child who imagined himself to be an adult; in actual fact, he was an adult who had remained a child. Already a grown man, he loved playing with tin and wooden soldiers, and he had no desire to know and understand the country he was destined to rule». Peter III went out of his way to emphasise his admiration for the Prussian king Frederick II and he habitually wore a Prussian uniform and Prussian decorations. He forced the Prussian uniform on the Russian army, formed a bodyguard of Holstein Germans and showed a marked preference for them over the Russian Guards.

It must be admitted, though, that Peter's first decrees made a good impression on society. The Secret Chancellery was abolished, the price of salt lowered, the rights of the gentry improved, the persecution of Old Believers prohibited. But these decrees were issued on the insistence of the Vorontsovs and the Shuvalovs, who sought to consolidate the position of the new emperor. Peter III himself had nothing to do with them. On April 24, 1762, he concluded a peace treaty with Frederick II that was greatly to Russia's disadvantage. He intended, in order to please the Prussian king, to declare war on Austria and Denmark, and he even relinquished the territories Russia had won in Eastern Prussia. All this made the Russians gnash their teeth in fury, the historian Bolotov testified. In other words, the Emperor of Russia behaved like a devoted subject of the Prussian king. In everyone's view he kissed the bust of Frederick II and knelt before his portrait and, conversely, flaunted his contempt for Russian Orthodox rituals. Through this behaviour and his neglect of the tasks of a ruler Peter III paved the way to the throne for his consort, Catherine. «All expected a coup», wrote Bolotov, «especially an attack on the Emperor on the part of the Guards.»

Emperor Paul I. Drawing.

On June 27, 1762, the Guards officer Alexei Orlov brought Peter's wife Catherine and her son Paul from the Peterhof to St. Petersburg. In front of the Kazan Cathedral gathered a large number of troops, and there and then Catherine was solemnly proclaimed Empress and her son, heir-apparent. The Senate and the Synod approved the Manifesto which pointed out that the administration of Peter III was incompatible with the interests of the state and the church.

The German princess Sophia Augusta Frederica of Anhalt-Zerbst was united in marriage with the future Russian Emperor Peter III on August 25, 1745. On adopting the Orthodox faith, she received the name Ekaterina Alexeyevna. She renounced her claim to the Anhalt-Zerbst Duchy and became preoccupied with her adopted mother-country, guided by a persistent feeling that she was going to play a great role in its destinies.

From the moment she appeared at the Russian court Catherine behaved with great circumspection. She made a good impression on Empress Elisabeth and her courtiers by her piety and punctilious observance of Orthodox rituals. The newlyweds had no affection for each other, and with time this dislike grew into hatred. Catherine worked assiduously on self-education, preparing herself for the role of ruler, and did everything possible to win the love of Russians. «I wish and want only good for the country to which God has brought me. Its glory will glorify me as well.»

On September 20, 1754, Catherine gave birth to a son, who was christened Paul. Subsequently she paid little attention to her child, and his upbringing was largely supervised by Empress Elisabeth.

Catherine, in the meantime, read modern European and classical literature. She was particularly fascinated by the works of Voltaire, spoke ecstatically of Montesquieu's «L'Esprit des lois» and worked to master the Encyclopaedia of Diderot and D'Alembert. She dreamed of initiating reforms in Russia, and to this end studied the legislation of European countries and matters of administration.

From the initial days of her reign, Catherine II showed herself to be resolute and painstaking. A proponent of absolute monarchy, she believed that the sovereign endowed with absolute power had a responsibility towards his subjects and that laws should further the popular wellbeing. After the coronation, Catherine II set to work on her Nakaz («Instructions»), which contained the principles of legislation which she wanted to enact in Russia. Humanist in essence, the Nakaz was acclaimed by Voltaire. The peak of Empress Catherine's legislative activity occurred in the period 1775-1785.

Catherine II was well aware of the evils inherent in serfdom. At the Free Economic Society she was instrumental in setting up she appointed an award of 10,000 gold roubles for the best essay advocating the abolition of serfdom. She repeatedly voiced the opinion that, if there were no opposition to the enslavement of the peasants, the state was bound for a crisis. Despite Catherine's good intentions, the abolition of serfdom was postponed until a century later. Moreover, the Empress was forced to act contrary to her humanitarian principles, in particular, to issue a decree that bound peasants to land in the Ukraine, and also to legalise the selling of individual serfs, even when the break-up of a family was involved.

In the 1770s Empress Catherine II was at the zenith of her glory and referred to herself as «the most aristocratic empress in Europe». Count Panin described the role of Russia in world politics at that time in these terms, «The world suddenly realised, much to its astonishment, that our (Russian) court had come to play an important role in the joint affairs of the greatest powers, and in the North it assumed the leading role.» Under Catherine II, interference of foreign powers in the affairs of the Russian

Empire became impossible, and the double-headed eagle spread its wings from Poland to China.

The annexation of the Crimea gave Russia an outlet to the Black and the Mediterranean Seas. The navy built by Prince Potyomkin won one victory after another over the Turks. Ochakov was captured. Suvorov routed the Turks at Focsani. Prince Repnin besieged Ismail. The Russians seized Gajibei, and in its place built the city of Odessa. Suvorov took Ismail by storm. Russia conducted its last war against Turkey at the same time as it fought Sweden. The king of Sweden Gustavus III intended to recapture the lands along the Baltic coast which Sweden had lost to Peter the Great, and boasted that he would topple the famous equestrian statue of Peter the Great in St. Petersburg. But the battle of Hogland demonstrated the strength of the Russian navy. On May 3, 1790, Admiral Chichagov won a decisive battle over the Swedes in the battle of Revel. In the peace negotiations that followed Russia did not cede an inch of its land to the Swedes. The wars, the toughening of serfdom, the increased taxation and the 25-year term of military service placed a heavy burden on the Russian peasantry and provoked several peasant rebellions. The biggest of these was one led by Yemelian Pugachov, who promised freedom to the peasants and repeal of Catherine's unpopular laws. The rebellion assumed the scope of a veritable peasant revolt, and it took Catherine much time and effort to suppress it.

At the end of her reign, Catherine II closely followed the revolutionary events in France. She regarded the French Revolution of 1789 as seizure of power by unlawful means, as the establishment of an unchristian idea and a «godless and seditious order». She wrote in this connection, «Equality is a monster, which aspires to become king by fair means or foul».

The French Revolution wrought a change in Catherine's internal and foregn policies. She aimed to set up a coalition in Europe against revolutionary France. Censorship and other restrictions were introduced in Russia. The Empress took harsh exception to the activities of the enlightener and publisher Nikolai Novikov and to Alexander Radischev's critical book «A Journey from Petersburg to Moscow». Both were severely punished.

The last years of Catherine's reign were clouded with grave emotional experiences. The Empress deeply mourned the death of Potyomkin and the failure of the betrothal of her granddaughter Alexandra Pavlovna to Gustavus IV, the king of Sweden. The marriage was cancelled at the last moment because the bridegroom and the bride belonged to different religious confessions.

On November 5, 1796 the Empress suddenly lost consciousness and died from paralysis.

During her reign it was rumoured that the Empress contemplated setting the accession of her son, Tsarevich Paul, aside in favour of her grandson Alexander. Her sudden death frustrated all these plans. Her son Paul acceded to the throne at the age of 42. In his mother's lifetime the tsarevich was in the position of her rival. She did not take part in his upbringing. Paul did not participate in state administration. The Empress did her best to prevent him from playing a role in administrative and military affairs. When Paul married the Grand Duchess of Wurttemberg (renamed Maria Fyodorovna when she became Empress) tensions between Catherine and the tsarevich's court came to a head. Paul and his wife could not forgive Catherine for having denied them the opportunity of bringing up their sons. Until the death of his mother Paul lived in the Gatchina Palace in seclusion.

Paul I had a different idea of autocratic rule from that of his mother. He strove to revive medieval respect for the autocratic rule of the tsar when

Emperor Alexander I. Drawing.

the state was regarded as his domain. The first act promulgated by Paul I introduced a statute on succession. Paul thought that stabilization of the order of succession was a prerequisite for a proper state structure. The Statute on the Imperial Family established the order of succession to the throne from father to the eldest son and in the case of a childless father to his eldest brother. Paul I decided to curb the self-rule of the nobility and gentry and cut the privileges of the higher estate causing discontent among the guards and in the court.

The French Revolution exercised a strong influence on Paul's foreign policy. Like Catherine, Paul was a fervent supporter of monarchy. He joined the coalition against France.

During the reign of Paul I the French quickly conquered Holland, Belgium, Switzerland and virtually all of Italy, and were preparing for a campaign against Egypt, establishing a republican order everywhere. The reason for the rupture of relations between France and Russia was the seizure by the French of the island of Malta which belonged to the Ionian knights under the protection of Russia.

At this time Russian troops, under the command of Suvorov, which had been sent to the aid of Austria, were operating in Northern Italy. This was Suvorov's famous Italian campaign. After capturing Milan and Turin the commander drove the French out of virtually all of Italy in one and a half months. In a three-day battle he routed Macdonald's army on the Tiber River and defeated Joubert's army in the valley near Mount Novi. After seizing all of Northern Italy Suvorov was making preparations for an offensive against France but at the request of Austria Paul I sent Russian troops to Switzerland. When the Russians departed the Austrians withdrew their troops. The Russian corps under the command of Rimski-Korsakov was left there alone. Suvorov rushed with his troops to its rescue and reached Lake Lucerne, where the French lay in wait for them. But Suvorov divined the enemy's plans and led his troops to safety across the forbidding mountain pass, fighting back the French. Suvorov's march across Switzerland won admiration in Europe. Paul I promoted Suvorov to the rank of generalissimo of the Russian Army.

Participation in the coalition was a bitter disappointment to Paul I. He understood that members of the coalition used the successes of the Russian Army for their own benefit. Suvorov cleared the French out of Italy but it was seized by Austria. England prevented Russia from recovering Malta. At that time, Napoleon used the achievements of the Revolution for his own purposes and laid the foundations for his imperial rule. Paul was one of the first to understand this metamorphosis. Seeing through his imperial leanings Paul joined him in an alliance and declared war on England.

In the early days of his reign Paul's ire and suspicions were attenuated by the influence of the Empress Maria Fyodorovna. But as time went by the extremes of his uncontrollable temper began to be felt by all those at court. Soon he found himself in tragic isolation. The Emperor strove to put things in order by using his unlimited power.

There are many jokes dating back to the rule of Paul I. But some of Paul's innovations were expedient. He took drastic measures to root out embezzlement in the army, and introduced individual training of soldiers in the field. This system took root.

The Emperor not only introduced ridiculous wigs in the army and tight-fitting footwear after the Prussian fashion but also stopped indulgence in luxury among officers of the Guards. Bolotov, Paul's contemporary, makes this assessment of his reforms of the army: «The first thing Paul did was...to wake up all Guards officers from their slumber and bliss. All had to give up their drowsiness and easy-going ways, get up very early, don their uniforms before daybreak...and, on a par with the other ranks, perform their duties every day...»

Paul also sought to eliminate abuses in the civilian administration. At the beginning of his reign there were up to 10,000 unresolved issues in the Senate. The Emperor put the officials to work. On his orders treasury bills worth five million roubles were burned before the Winter Palace. In this way the value of money was increased. In four years of his rule the Emperor did a lot of things. He slashed salt prices, increased the country's grain stocks, initiated work on forest conservation, established trade relations with America, inaugurated the Russian-American company and set up a higher medical school.

Senior officials were set against Paul for his pursuit of embezzlers, Guards for the introduction of strict discipline in the army and its officer corps, the nobility for the curtailment of its rights. The Manifesto of 1797 limited the work of serfs for their overlords to three days per week. Every serf could write directly to the tsar and the latter opened the post box with letters himself.

Catherine II was far from being doctrinaire. «The passion for systematic thinking gives rise to stubbornness and intransigence and to the urge to persecute others,» she wrote. Paul did not take heed of these behests of his mother. Sometimes strict compliance with his orders was carried too far. For example, he banned wearing wide-brimmed hats in St. Petersburg. In fact, they were ordered to be snatched off and torn on the spot. Round hats reminded Paul of the fashions of revolutionary France and he flew into a rage when he saw anything resembling antimonarchical ideas. Owing to his emotional outbursts Paul lost many loyal followers. He suspected everyone surrounding him of conspiring against him. In spite of his circumspection, he appointed General Pahlen who was, in fact, the driving power in the conspiracy against him, to the post of military governor of St.Petersburg. Paul was murdered in the bedroom of the St.Michael Palace.

Alexander I, the eldest son of Paul I and Empress Maria Fyodorovna, acceeded to the throne.

Catherine II, who doted on her grandson, took care of his education and upbringing. When the tsarevich was four years old she began to teach him arithmetic, wrote children's books for him and encouraged his reading. She was impressed with his abilities. In spite of her love of the tsarevich he spent his young years in a complicated environment. He had to mix in two courts—Catherine's «big» Petersburg court and the «small» Gatchina court where his father and mother lived. The sensitive tsarevich absorbed many negative emotions from his early observations of court life. In 1796, Alexander wrote to his tutor La Harpe: «There is an incredible disarray at the St.Petersburg court, thieving is rampant, all its parts are badly managed.» He was sharply critical of Catherine's favouritism and pandering to her entourage. In contrast to the loose morals of the Petersburg Palace strict discipline and order reigned supreme at the Gatchina court. They did not discuss the ideas of «enlightened absolutism» with their rationality and Voltaireanism in Gatchina but stood firmly by religious ethics and the values of «common sense and faith». The maturing tsarevich formed his own opinion which was different from that of those who surrounded him but he had to conceal it. Count Panin and Pahlen who initiated the conspiracy against Paul I, brought pressure to bear on the Tsarevich to make him agree to their plan for forcing his father to abdicate from the throne. Alexander consented on condition that they would do no harm to the Emperor. Count Pahlen gave this promise but did not keep it.

Karamzin summed up the prevailing sentiments in society after Alexander I succeeded to the throne as follows: «Two opinions were uppermost in the minds of people at that time. Some wanted Alexander, in his eternal glory, to take measures to curb the unlimited autocratic rule so ruinous under his parent; others doubted the success of this enterprise and wanted him only to re-establish the destroyed system of Catherine's reign which was so happy and wise compared with Paul's system».

Upon acceding to the throne Alexander I said that he was at one «in mind and heart with my grandmother Catherine». In the early years of his reign Alexander sought to achieve two objectives: to free the Emperor's rule from its dependence on the capital's nobility and officialdom and ensure the unity of the empire by its complete integration with Poland and Finland. Alexander I was a child of his time, the Age of Enlightenment. He sought to merge the fundamentals of monarchical power with the principles of freedom and equality. This programme took shape in 1804 and was the basis of his international policy. Alexander was carried away by his far-reaching plans for restructuring his empire and Europe on fundamentally new principles.

Karamzin pointed out that Alexander's accession to the throne delighted the nobility. In her reminiscences a contemporary wrote: «Alexander Pavlovich was so handsome and attractive that he eclipsed everybody in court ballrooms and the Empress could not help admiring him. The Empress was also beautiful when she was young but later she lost her good looks and red spots appeared on her face but she was loved by her entourage and courtiers for her kindness and simplicity. She lived a virtuous life beyond reproach. She was like those faithful tsarinas of the ancient world who were canonized saints.

«There were people who blamed Alexander Pavlovich for being insincere. I cannot be a judge. What I know is that in spite of his romantic infatuations he was a man of integrity. He was pious from his young years and sometimes told people close to him that he would like to leave everything behind and became a monk.»

Alexander planned to introduce the rule of law in the state and, for this purpose, adopt new «fundamental» laws which were absent in Russia. In the early days of his reign the Emperor created what was later called a «privy committee» to draft reforms. It included talented and well-educated young men who were well-versed in the state structure of the West-Count Victor P. Kochubei, Count Pavel A. Stroganov, Nikolai N. Novosiltsev, and the Polish Count Adam Czartoryski.

Stroganov wrote: «The Emperor acceded to the throne with the best of intentions of establishing order on as firm a foundation as possible. He planned to draft laws for restructuring the state and social system and improving education, production and culture. The peasant question was also raised even though it was tackled timidly». He went on to say: «The peasants constitute a class on which attention should be focused in Russia; this numerous class consists of people who for the most part are endowed with high intellect and enterprise but, being deprived of the right to freedom and property, they are doomed to eke out a miserable existence; they do not make a contribution for the benefit of society by the labour of which they are capable; they have no firm status or property».

The government took the first steps towards the abolition of serfdom. On December 12, 1801, the Emperor's birthday, a decree was promulgated permitting all those on estates to buy land. Some landlords began to sell their land to peasants. On February 20, 1803 a decree to free ploughmen was issued. A landlord could negotiate with peasants and set free whole villages and families with land.

The beginning of the war with Napoleon in 1805 and subsequent military setbacks interrupted the liberal domestic reforms. Alexander was deserted by his younger supporters. Their place was taken by Mikhail M. Speransky, a talented and industrious man, who drafted a system of reform of the Russian state.

Speransky's plan of constitutional reform was based on the division of legislative, executive and judicial power and recognition of civil rights. The reform of local government was a central issue. But political changes had to be preceded by economic transformation if the reform was to bring permanent benefits and provoke no upheavals. Later Speransky's plan was rejected. It was regarded as undermining the autocracy. The Emperor also tended to share this view.

Alexander contemplated creating a confederation of all European states on the principles of international law and national justice. The beginning of the nineteenth century in Europe was marked by the crumbling of illusions about Napoleon. The «fraternity of peoples» proclaimed by the Great French Revolution turned in the hands of the dictator into the subjugation of European states to French domination.

Alexander's mammoth plan for a confederation of all European states based on principles of national justice and international law was blocked by Napoleon who placed many states in Europe under his sway. Napoleon reaffirmed his power in the famous Battle of Austerlitz. Alexander saw the danger hovering over his empire. He decided to come to terms with the usurper and on June 25-26, 1807 an alliance of eternal friendship was signed in Tilsit where the two emperors met on a raft in the middle of the River Neman. Russia had to join the «continental blockade» of Britain, which adversely affected its trade, but Alexander did not abandon his plans of uniting Europe.

In 1810, the government received information that Napoleon was making preparations for war against Russia. The war broke out in 1812. Fierce fighting, such as at the Battle of Borodino, the burning of Moscow, a national uprising and the retreat of Napoleon's army took place without Alexander's direct participation. Mikhail I. Kutuzov led the army. The victory of the Russian people opened the way for Alexander in 1814 to implement his concept of organizing Europe on a new, peaceful basis. After evicting Napoleon from Russia Kutuzov and his generals were in favour of signing a peace favourable to Russia. But Alexander stood his grounds. «If we want to have an honourable and durable peace it has to be signed in Paris.» Alexander was with the Russian army all the way from Wilno to Paris. In September 1815, acting in concert with the Austrian Emperor and Prussian king, he signed the Holy Alliance Act, which he had drafted himself. It expressed the will to be guided in international and domestic affairs at the «behests of holy faith, the eternal law guiding the will of tsars».

Alexander referred to the Alliance of Four Powers as «Christian convention». «I hope sincerely,» he wrote, «that sometime all denominations will merge, I believe it quite possible, but the time has not come yet». This idea had to be the foundation of fraternal unity of peoples and governments in the Holy Alliance. In the 1820s the Holy Alliance reaffirmed by the Paris Treaty of 1818 faced a crisis. Neither England nor the Pope supported Alexander's initiatives. The «Christian convention» was denounced in Rome as «an attempt by the Emperor of an Orthodox state to lead the Christian world».

In the 1820s Alexander I was torn by inner contradictions.

His contemporaries described the last years of his life as a «protracted clouding of his mind.» He gave up his plans for reform, refusing to carry them out, and left the administration of the state to Arakcheyev. There was no longer any talk of reforms or the desire to introduce the principles of the Holy Alliance in Russia.

In actual fact Alexander lived his life in isolation. During his reign his mother, dowager Maria Fyodorovna, played the role of the Empress exercising a strong influence on Alexander. His wife, Elizaveta Alexeyevna, did not play a significant part in public or private life.

His married life with Maria Naryshkina (née Princess Czetwertynska) isolated Alexander to a large extent from public interests. The death of their 18-year old daughter in 1824 impaired the health of the Emperor. He was often heard saying that he wanted to abdicate. Pessimistic moods overwhelmed him. His reminiscences of the assassination of his father and pricks of conscience left a deep scar on him. He died in Taganrog.

The Emperor Alexander I died childless and the throne should have passed to his elder brother Constantine Pavlovich who was the viceroy of the Kingdom of Poland. But Constantine Pavlovich, who was married to a Polish princess Joanna Grudzinska, had renounced his claims to the throne earlier. The Emperor accepted his abdication on the grounds that members of the Romanov dynasty could only marry members of royal families or else they were deprived of their dynastic rights.

But the manifesto on the abdication of Constantine was not proclaimed in the lifetime of Alexander I and was kept secret even from the Grand Duke Nikolai Pavlovich. After the death of Alexander I the packages containing the abdication documents were opened in keeping with the will of the late Emperor. Nikolai Pavlovich had the right to imperial succession but he did not think it possible to be crowned in the absence of his brother Constantine and hoped that the latter would confirm his abdication in person. In the meantime, the Russian capital followed by the whole of Russia took the oath to Constantine and the latter, in accordance with his abdication statement, took the oath to Nicholas. He planned to go to St. Petersburg to reaffirm his abdication. The confusion in the imperial family did not go unnnoticed by the population.

At that time, members of secret revolutionary societies, later referred to as

Palace of the Romanov boyars. Drawing.

Decembrists, rose to overthrow autocratic rule and establish a republican form of government.

Constantine Pavlovich reiterated his abdication but refused to come to St. Petersburg. Then the Emperor Nicholas I issued a manifesto on January 14, 1825 announcing his accession to the throne and called on the troops and the population to take the oath of allegiance to him. Part of the soldiers did not take the oath and stood in formation at the monument to Peter the Great on Senate Square. The Emperor Nicholas I pitted regiments of the Guard against them. Count Miloradovich, St.Petersburg's governor, rode to the mutinous regiments in order to speak to them but was shot and killed by Kakhovsky, one of the leaders of the mutiny. Then armed force was used against the mutineers.

The December events of 1825 affected all subsequent activities of Nicholas I. In the course of the enquiry into the case of the Decembrists he supervised the work of the investigating commission in person, predetermined the sentence, followed the lives of exiled Decembrists in remote Siberia and decided all questions relatives to their destiny.

On the Emperor's orders the investigating commission probing into the case of the Decembrists studied the reasons which had led to the uprising. Conclusions were also drawn on the tasks Nicholas I had to tackle first. «It is necessary to make clearly formulated positive laws, establish justice by instituting speedy judicial process, improve the ethical education of the clergy, support the gentry who fall on hard times and are bled white by loans in credit institutions, revive trade and industry, improve the status of the tillers of the soil and abolish humiliating trade in human beings». Nicholas always had the list of these conclusions and comments at hand. Characteristically, in the manifesto Nicholas issued after his reprisals against the Decembrists he wrote that the need for reform would be met «not by catering to insolent wishful thinking, which is always destructive, but through improvement of the existing order by the government».

Many historians believe that since Alexander I had not made up his mind and the Decembrists failed to carry out revolutionary changes in the country Nicholas I, undoubtedly, acted as a «revolutionary from above», emphasising the continuity of Peter's line in every way. But his attempt at reform failed because of the strong and ever growing opposition of officialdom, the bureaucracy and nobility. Nicholas feared that the abolition of serfdom would lead to the establishment of a bourgeois constitutional system. He thought he was duty bound to keep the Russian autocratic system intact. Nicholas used to say that he received his Emperor's crown unexpectedly, that he was destined to rule Russia and that he had to safeguard and strengthen it and hand it over to his successor as a strong power. Model military discipline and firm religious principles were his first priority.

Moscow. The Kremlin.
Interior of the Archangel Cathedral.

Family Tree
of the Romanovs. Icon.

Moscow. The Kremlin. Shrine of the Russian tsars in the Archangel Cathedral.

Left : The Armoury. Gospel cover. Gold, enamel, jewels. By U. Frobos and others.1686. Moscow. The Kremlin. Paintings of the Tsarina's Golden Chamber.

Right : The Terem Palace. The Armoury. Gilded golden saddle. By Ionov. 17th century.

The Terem Palace in the Kremlin.

Gilded saddle. Ionov, master saddler. The Armury, 17th century.

28

The Armoury. Diadem.

*The Armoury.
Russian armour.
12-19th centuries.*

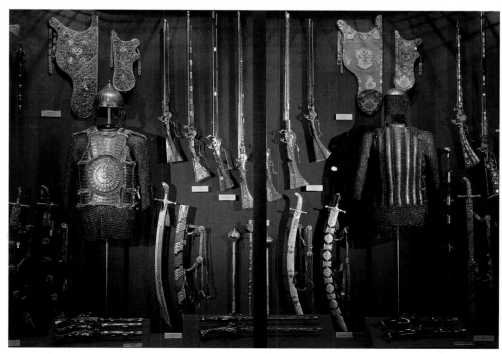

*The Armoury. Helmet.
Sigismund's gift to
Tsar Fyodor. 1591.*

Diamond Fund.
«Orlov Diamond».

Triptych icon.
17-18th centuries.

The Armoury. Cassock. Detail. Gold-thread embroidery, pearls.

The Armoury. Easter gold egg decorated with diamonds and rubies. Fabergé 1902.

The Armoury. Goblet of tsar Ivan Alekseevich.
Late 17th century.

The Armoury. Silver dish. 1685.

The Armoury. Gilded silver ladle.
Late 16th century.

Gold chalice decorated with jewels. 1668.

Moscow. The Grand Kremlin Palace.

The Armoury. Crown of Empress Anne. 1730

The Armoury. Bouquet. 18th century.

The Armoury. Enamels. 17th century.

State Seal of Peter the Great.
Moscow. The Kremlin. The Terem Palace.

Next pages : Moscow Kremlin at night.

ALEXANDER II

1818 - 1881

*Emperor Alexander II
with his daughter Grand Duchess
Maria. 1870s*

*Opposite: Sebastopol.
View of the southern bay from Bastion
No.4. 1856. Phototype*

Aleksandr Nikolaevich was born in the Moscow Kremlin on April 17, 1818. He was the eldest son of Emperor Nicholas I and his wife Aleksandra Fyodorovna. Tsarevich Alexander had Vassily Zhukovsky, a prominent Russian poet, as his tutor. It was Zhukovsky himself who had elaborated a special humanitarian course for the heir apparent which included studies in world and Russian history, ancient and European languages, history of art and literature, law, economics, etc. Zhukovsky's credo was formulated in one of his poems in which appealing to the heir apparent he wrote, «You have to be a Man on the throne». His tutors in military science were a brave officer Captain K.K. Merder and Lieutenant General P.P. Ushakov who instilled into Alexander's mind an idea of gentle and humane rule.

Tsarevich Alexander was a man of common sense, possessed both of a firm character and sensitive heart. Both Alexander and his father were interested in military science : Emperor Nicholas considered military study to be the main part of his son's education. So it was an occupation after Alexander's own heart. Moreover at the age of 18, the Tsarevich succeeded in commanding the Preobrazhensky and Hussars regiments at manoeuvres.

In 1837, his all-round education was completed. After passing his examinations Alexander accompanied by Zhukovsky travelled a good deal through the whole of Russia in order to learn about the conditions of the Russian people. The suffering of the Siberian exiles filled him with sorrow and he interceded with his father for the improvement of their state. Emperor Nicholas complied with the Tsarevich's request.

In 1838, Alexander and Zhukovsky visited Europe. In Darmstadt, Alexander met his future wife, fifteen-year-old princess Maria of Hesse Darmstadt. On April 16, 1841 Alexander married Maria who had been baptized into the Orthodox Church and become Maria Alexandrovna. They had two daughters and five sons. Alexander II ascended the throne on February 19, 1855 on the sudden death of his father emperor Nicholas I at the height of the Crimean War.

The Crimean War continued. In the autumn of 1855 Russian troops sustained a defeat in Sebastopol. Although it was followed by the Russian invasion of Kars, the main Turkish fortress, this didn't change the overall situation. According to the peace treaty that concluded the Crimean War in Paris on March 18, 1856, Russia got Sevastopol back in return for Kars but was refused Moldavia at the mouth of the Danube. Russia was also forbidden to have a Black Sea Fleet. These restrictions were lifted only in 1871 during the Franco-Prussian War of 1870-1871. It was only victory in the Russo-Turkish War that gave Russia the opportunity to restore her rights to their full extent.

In 1876, Alexander II published a special manifesto to declare both the end of the Crimean War and the beginning of the reforms the country had need of. Alexander decided to make the social reorganization his father had failed to fulfill.

So the «era of Great Reforms» of Alexander II began. He started with the abolition of serfdom. This reform is no doubt considered to be the most important and the starting-point for the next reforms. On February 19,1861 Alexander II published «Act of Emancipation» according to which serfdom, the system the majority of Russian population had been living under for almost 300 years, was abolished. It was this act that won for emperor Alexander II the epithet «Tsar Liberator». The manifesto permitted peasants to buy land. For these purposes the government granted 49- year loans, but all the loans were paid off in 20 years. The result was that during the first ten years after the abolition of serfdom the grain market in Russia, her main export, increased by 70 %. The Act of Emancipation was rapidly followed by administrative and judicial reforms. The first one was aimed at reorganizing the organs of general goverment for rural districts. Elective local assemblies, so called «zemstva», were established. Their area of self-government included local industry, trade, railways, education, medical care, etc. Judicial reform was aimed at the reorganization of the judicial administration on the basis of progressive European practice which included the principles of publication, elected representatives, independent judiciary, trial by jury, etc. Judicial authority was separated from the administration. Alexander II was convinced that the Court of Law in Russia had to be « fast, just, merciful and equal for all subjects». The same system was established in the army.

A democratic system of universal military training was introduced by the manifesto published on January 1, 1874. It read, «Defence of the throne and fatherland is a sacred duty of every Russian, therefore young men of all classes are liable to do military service». The problem was to change the attitude to military service. Corporal punishment was also abolished by the manifesto.

Some measures were taken to improve the educational system. Russian universities received rights of self-government. New universities were opened in Odessa and Warsaw. The restrictions concerning the social position or religion of children who wanted to attend high schools were lifted. High schools for girls, further education for women and schools for nurses were opened. Further measures were taken to improve the system of primary education which included the establishment of a large number of primary schools. During Alexander II's reign the number of schools increased. So Alexander's reforms applied to almost every sphere of Russian life. They were of great social value and improved the general condition of the country.

Alexander II's reign policy was aimed at the improvement of Russia's international position. At this time, a second national rebellion in Poland was suppressed. It was followed by measures undertaken to change the situation in Poland. On February 19, 1864 Alexander II passed an edict to give Polish peasants ownership of their land. Russian money was used to pay off the former landowners for their lands.

In 1864, the Caucasus became a part of Russia. The war between the mountain-dwellers and the Russian army which had been waged continuously from the beginning of 19th century came to an end. The mountain-dwellers decided to surrender and declare their loyalty to the Russian emperor. Meanwhile Russia was extending domination in Asia in order to strengthen her Asian borders. The establishment of the protectorate of Bukhara in 1868 and Khiva in 1873 was followed by the abolition of slavery there.

At the same time Alexander was anxious about a danger which might have threatened from Great Britain. There was no doubt that the extension of the area of Russian domination in Asia made trouble for both Great Britain and France. In 1875, there was a rebellion of Slav people in Turkey. Soon Bosnia and Herzegovina joined them. Attempts at peaceful negotiation ended in failure. Inspired by public opinion Alexander II decided to become the champion of the oppressed Slav people. On April 12, 1877 Russia declared war on Turkey.

From the very beginning of the war, the emperor was in the Danube Army in the field. He said, «I am going to be a male nurse». He visited the hospitals where the Russian wounded men were being treated and tried to cheer them up.

In the middle of May, the Commander-in-Chief Grand Duke Nikolai Nikolaevich informed the emperor about a forthcoming crossing of the Danube. Because of the rain followed by spring floods the crossing was postponed but took place later on June 15. The real war now began.

At first, the Russian attack was crowned with success. On July 7, Trnovo, a former Bulgarian capital, surrendered. Inspired by success, the Russian army believed in a forthcoming victory. Constantinople was expected to be captured soon, and a Russian soldier was to put the Orthodox cross on the dome of St. Sophia's Cathedral. As Fyodor Tyuchev expressing his pan-slavic idea wrote in a political poem, «Isn't it high time Russia tolled the bell in Tsargrad?» However, the war Russia had become involved in proved more painful that might have seemed at first sight. The situation changed. The Russian army was totally defeated in three battles for the city of Plevna and the siege following it which began in the autumn of 1877 cost Russia great loss of life. In spite of the winter coming and the beginning of epidemic of cholera and typhoid, the headquarters of the army persisted in continuing the siege of Plevna. Alexander refused to come back to St. Petersburg. He said, «I won't leave my army until Plevna has surrendered».

It happened on November 28, 1877. The Turkish army led by Osman Pasha surrendered. Victory in the war was ensured.

Alexander II came back to St. Petersburg on December 18,1877. He received a great welcome there. Everybody could see how the war had told on his appearance. As one of his contemporaries wrote, «At the time the war began Alexander was a tall and handsome man, maybe a little bit stout. When he came back one looked in vain for his previous healthy appearance. Alexander had turned into a middle-aged man with sad eyes. He was so lean that it seemed he was only skin and bone. He has become old in a short period of time.»

Meanwhile, the Russian army led by Grand Duke Nicholas Romanov got across the Balkan Mountains. In spite of the severe winter, the Russian soldiers were full of enthusiasm. This manoeuvre opened the door to Constantinople. The Sultan was going to appeal for peace. At the same time, the appearance of the Russian army on the shores of the Mediterranean Sea made Great Britain move her fleet to Constantinople.

The treaty that concluded the Russo-Turkish war of 1877-1878 was signed on March 3, 1878 in the city of St. Stefano on the shore of the Sea of Marmora. Under the treaty Batumi, and Kars were annexed to Russia and Bessarabia, which Russia had lost after the Crimean War, was returned. Besides that Bulgaria, Serbia, Chernogoria and Romania became independent from Turkey. But under the pressure of Great Britain and Austria the treaty was reconsidered. A new one was concluded at the Congress of the European powers in Berlin on July 13,1878. Through that treaty Bosnia and Herzegovina was annexed to Austria-Hungary.

Nevertheless, as a result of the war, Chernogoria, Serbia and Bulgaria won the independence from Turkey in spite of some territorial concessions. As for Alexander II he won the epithet of «Tsar Liberator» for the second time.

At the end of the 1870s, there was a spate of revolutionary terrorism in Russia. On April 1, 1879 there was an attempt upon the life of the emperor. The terrorist Solovyov attempted to shoot Alexander II during his daily morning walk near the Winter Palace.

Although Alexander didn't hold extreme views on policy, urgent measures to stop terrorism were undertaken. They included the introduction of martial law for the districts and cities where acts of terrorism had taken place. The heads of the local administrations of St. Petersburg, Moscow, Kiev, Kharkov and Odessa were delegated a special authority for exterminating terrorist groups. Nevertheless the situation improved only for a short period of time.

The first attempt on the tsar's life was followed by a second one in November 19, 1880 when the train in which Alexander was going to Moscow was blown up. The tsar's life was saved by chance. Alexander exclaimed in despair, «What do these horrible people want from me? Why are they persecuting me?» Nothing could stop the assassins from trying to kill Alexander II. An explosion organized by S. Khalturin in the Winter Palace came next. As the famous French writer Melchior Vogue, who was the secretary of the French Embassy in Moscow at this time, wrote, «One couldn't describe the feeling of horror and instability that dominated the society. Rumours were being spread about possible new explosions in certain parts of St. Petersburg on February 19, 1880 (the Act of Emancipation anniversary). People were anxious and moved elsewhere and some left the city entirely. Neither the police nor the government could do anything. There was no doubt a strong expectation of a new power. A new saviour was expected». Meanwhile, new social reforms were being prepared by Alexander II that met the domestic needs of Russia. They included the abolition of the Third Section of the Imperial Police, reduction of administrative and censorship restrictions, further extension of the area of self-goverment of rural districts and cities and at least the establishment of legislative commissions with elected representatives. This last reform was of great importance because it could have opened the door to democracy in Russia.

Count Mikhail Loris-Melikov offered Alexander II his own programme of future reforms that combined both the idea of a strong autocratic power and the idea of further liberalization. He said to Alexander, «authority for governmental affairs must be placed in the hands of a trusted adviser». Alexander answered, «You shall be this man». Mikhail Loris-Melikov was also at the head of the Supreme Commission charged with exterminating the terrorist organizations and maintaining order in the country. The reforms were expected to start at the beginning of March 1881. The day before March 1, 1881 Alexander was informed of the danger of a new attempt upon his life. He was warned against going to the changing of the guard, a ritual he used to attend each Sunday morning. But Alexander insisted saying, «Why shouldn't I go to the ceremony as usual ?»

It happened at 2 p.m. on Alexander's way home to the Winter Palace near the St Michael Castle. A young man passing by suddenly threw a package at the tsar's carriage.The bomb in the package exploded, killing a number of the tsar's companions but Alexander himself was safe and sound. He tried to help the wounded men and then approached the terrorist. Suddenly, another bomb exploded. It was this second bomb thrown by another assassin that wounded Alexander mortally. After the explosion he was seen lying in a pool of blood with his legs injured. The Emperor was taken to the Winter Palace where he died two hours later.

The tragic death of Tsar Alexander II at the hands of assassins strengthened the conservative convictions of the new emperor Alexander III and his entourage who has disapproved of a policy of democratic reforms that might have led, they thought, to destruction of the God-given autocratic power the Russian tsars had inherited.

Melchior Vogue was among those people who greatly appreciated the policy Emperor Alexander II had pursued. He wrote, «Look at this great martyr! He was no doubt a great tsar and had deserved a lot better. Never was a life more completely devoted to the needs of his people, including the unfortunate and insulted ones... Remember his reforms! Maybe Peter the Great hadn't done more ... Remember all the hardships he had to overcome in order to abolish serfdom and create new conditions for the futher development of the Russian economy. Think of those 30 million peasants who were given their personal freedom... His administrative reforms were aimed at the reduction of class privileges and social injustice. The results of judicial reform were the establishment of independent judicial rights and the abolition of corporal punishment. He also strengthened the Russian position abroad. He realized the plans Catherine II had dreamed of. He improved the military condition of Russia and strengthened the Black Sea Fleet. He abolished the humiliating clauses of the Paris treaty. He brought the Russian army to the shores of the Sea of Marmora and helped Bulgaria to win independence. He extended Russian domination in Asia. On the very day of his death Alexander II was working on a reorganization project that could have been his best policy to date. It was a draft Constitution that might have led Russia to further humanitarian progress and peaceful economic development.

And that was the day he was assassinated by a bomb thrown by revolutionaries. The Cathedral of the Resurrection of Our Saviour on the Blood was built on the spot where Alexander II was assassinated.

Emperor Nicholas I.

«*Nobody was better suited for the role of an autocrat. He had the necessary appearance and moral qualities. The imposing and magnificent good looks, the haughty carriage, the regular Olympic profile, the imperious gaze - all, ending with the smile of a condescending Jupiter, which bespoke a deity, an all-powerful sovereign, all reflected a steadfast conviction of his eminent station. This man had never been assailed by even a shadow of doubt as to his power or its lawfulness. He believed in it with the blind faith of a fanatic, and the unquestioning passive obedience which he exacted from his subjects he was himself the first to offer to the ideal, which he considered himself obliged to embody in his person...*

«*As with every fanatic, his mental scope was restricted to an amazing degree by his moral convictions. He would not, and even could not, allow for anything that stood outside the range of concepts of which he had built a cult.*»

Anna Tyutcheva
From «Recollections» (of Nicholas I)

Sebastopol. Ruins of the city during the Crimean War. 1856.

«The same lack of thought which has laid a stamp on our political mode of action is also characteristic of our military management. It could not be otherwise. Suppression of thought has long been the guiding principle of our government. The consequences of such a system are limitless. Nothing has been spared. The pressure has put its stamp on everything. All and sundry have been stupefied...»

Fyodor Tyutchev.

Sebastopol. Charge against the Malakhov burial mound during the Crimean War. Lithograph.

Sebastopol. Fire on the embankment, June 9, 1855. Lithograph.

«At the very beginning of the Crimean War, the army - which had seemed so strictly disciplined - proved to lack good weapons and ammunition, to have been plundered by the commanders' graft and bribe-taking, and to be led by generals lacking initiative and military knowledge; all that remained was the courage and the loyalty of its soldiers, who were able to die but not retreat where they were unable to win because of the shortage of the means of defence and attack. The finances proved to have been exhausted, the means of transportation across the vast empire unusable, and in launching every new enterprise the state power came across difficulties created by corruption and thievery. Within a mere eighteen months, the unfortunate Emperor witnessed the foundations of the illusory grandeur, to which he imagined he had elevated Russia, crumble under his feet.»

Anna Tyutcheva, «Recollections»

Tsarevich Nikolai Aleksandrovich (sitting left) among people close to him. 1860s.

*Sebastopol. Dugout of Bastion No.3.
1856 (?).
Phototype from photo.*

*Sebastopol battery. 1856 (?).
Phototype from photo.*

*Sebastopol. Crimean War. Fedyunin Heights
and Traktirny Bridge.*

50

Alexander II with his son Paul. Early 1860s.

Empress Maria Aleksandrovna. 1860s.

«The Empress undoubtedly has great acumen; her mind is very subtle, very sensitive, very astute, but... She is much more suited to the life of the heart and the mind than for active work and external manifestations. She turns her ambition not to the attainment of power or political influence, but to the development of her inner being.»

Anna Tyutcheva. «Recollections»

«His main gift was a warm, ardent, humane heart, which naturally drew him to all that was generous and high-minded and impelled him to the great things that were accomplished during his reign... His heart had an instinct for progress, that was feared by his mind. His heart bled for the serfs, and he granted freedom to 18 million people... His heart was outraged by the bribery and the maladministration of justice, and he granted Russia new legal institutions. But later, when the current of life swept across the dam he himself had demolished... the bold reformer, dismayed and grieved, became frightened of his own great deed, tried to disown it, and to protect the order whose foundations he had himself undermined».

Anna Tyutcheva. «Recollections»

Alexander II. St. Petersburg. 1864.

Alexander II. Tsarskoe Selo. 1863.

*Left : Grand Dukes Sergei and Paul,
sons of Alexander II.
Crimea. 1863.*

*Right : Grand Duke
Nikolai Aleksandrovich, the eldest son
of Alexander II. Early 1860s.*

*Left : Grand Dukes Alexis
and Vladimir, sons of Alexander II.
St. Petersburg. 1864.*

*Right : Grand Duchess
Maria Aleksandrovna,
daughter of Alexander II.
St. Petersburg. 1864.*

Alexander II with his sons. 1860s.

Alexander II. Tsarskoe Selo. 1865.

Alexander II. 1860s.

*Alexander I with his daughter Maria and son Sergei.
Tsarskoe Selo. 1863.*

*«That evening I was with her when little
Maria Aleksandrovna, chirping like a little
bird, was brought in by the nurse. The Tsar
came in, the little darling stretched out her
arms to him, and he picked her up tenderly. It
was heart-warming to see them so kind and
loving, just like ordinary good people, to see
them made of the same human clay...»*

Anna Tyutcheva. «Recollections»

Alexander II with his daughter Maria and son Alexis. Mid-1860s.

Orphanage in Veyernoye.
Founded in 1879.

Preparations for the Eastern War of 1877-78.

Construction of railway.

«Alexander Nikolayevich Romanov was not born under a lucky star. Neither his reforms nor his military feats gave him those laurels which more fortunate people earned without trying very hard. Even his near ones, those who loved him sincerely, placed no confidence in him. During the Turkish campaign, Alexander Nikolayevich, exhausted by disease and moral shocks, lost weight, became stooped and pinched in face, and witnesses of his life at that time were unanimous in saying that he aroused pity... To the end of his days, Alexander II never learnt to wear the imperial crown.»

G. Chulkov. «Emperors»

Welcoming the Grenadier Corps on its return from the campaign of 1877-78.

*Left : Grand Duke Mikhail
Nikolayevich, brother of Alexander II.
Crimea. 1863.*

*Right : Anastasia, daughter of
the Grand Duke Mikhail Nikolayevich.
Tiflis. 1865.*

*Mikhail Nikolayevich Romanov, the fourth
son of the Emperor Nicholas I, was born on
October 13, 1832. After accession to the throne
of Alexander II the Grand Duke was appointed
member of the State Council. In 1856 he became
Chief of Artillery. He married the Grand
Duchess Olga Fyodorovna in the same year.*

*Left : Olga Fyodorovna, wife
of the Grand Duke
Mikhail Nikolayevich. England. 1861.*

*Right : Grand Duke
Constantine Nikolayevich,
brother of Alexander II. 1864.*

Konstantin Nikolayevich Romanov, the second son of the Emperor Nicholas I, was born on September 9, 1827. All his life was closely linked with the navy. In 1844 he made his first tour abroad. Six years later he was appointed a member of the State Council, chairman of the committee for drafting a navy manual. In 1853, the Grand Duke was put in charge of the Admiralty. Konstantin Nikolayevich enthuasiastically supported all the reforms of Alexander II.

Konstantin Nikolayevich with his wife and children. 1860s. (Person on the right is unidentified).

*Russian ambassador to Turkey
Nikolai P. Ignatiev working on the
Treaty of San Stefano with Turkey
in a mountain hut. 1878.*

«*Alexander II has achieved a great deal, a
very great deal; his name already now rises
above those of all his predecessors. In the name
of human rights, in the name of compassion, he
fought against a predatory mob of crass scoun-
drels and overpowered them. Neither the
Russian people, nor world history will ever for-
get this. From our far-away exile, we hail him
and bestow on him a name that has rarely been
bestowed on an autocrat without a bitter smile
- we hail him as a LIBERATOR...*»
Alexander Herzen

Alexander II. Late 1870s.
Photo by Levitsky.

ALEXANDER III

1845 - 1894

*Tsarevich Alexander Aleksandrovich
with his wife Maria and son Nikolai.
St. Petersburg. Late 1860s.
Photo by Levitsky.*

*Left : Arrival of the Emperor
Alexander III in Moscow. 1891.*

After the assassination of Tsar Alexander II the autocratic power passed to his son Alexander. Aleksandr Aleksandrovich was born on February 25, 1845 in St. Petersburg. He was the second son of Alexander II. His elder brother, Tsarevich Nikolai Aleksandrovich, died on April 12, 1865. Alexander became heir apparent after the death of his brother. Alexander was deeply attached to Nicholas from his childhood, he was his first friend and confidant. The death of Nicholas made a deep impression on him.

Alexander III received a traditional classical education. There were prominent historians and a philologist among his tutors such as S. Solovyov, F. Buslaev, and J. Grot.

Alexander was interested in Russian history and art. He was considered to be an expert in archaeology and especially iconography. He was an active member of the Russian Historical Society that had been founded under his auspices and took part in the compiling of the Russian Biographical Encyclopaedia.

He studied the principles of law under the reactionary minister K.P. Pobedonostsev. Pobedonostsev was a very significant figure in the history of Russia. From 1880 till the end of his life he was Procurator of the Holy Synod and determined the policy of Russia to a great extent. He had also a profound influence upon Alexander III himself.

Pobedonostsev's outlook opposed Russian culture to European culture. It was based on the complete negation of both decent human nature and rationalism, fundamental ideas which Western-European culture believed in. He blamed rationalism for its, as he supposed, schematicism which had nothing in common with real historical process. As for believing in the decent human nature of man, this idea had produced democracy and parlamentarianism which, according to Pobedonostsev, were nothing but «a great lie of our time».

His conservative ideology condemned the idea of widespread popular education. He believed that education could give a certain knowledge, teach a proper way of thinking, but failed to play any significant role in the real life of people. He warned against life being submitted to rationalism. He wrote, «The only significant quality of a human being is intuition. In spite of the fact that they often treat it as foolishness and ignorance, intuition is without doubt of great importance for the whole of society. It is based on a strong belief in God, which has nothing in common with diverse theories and intellectual efforts. Faith is far better than knowledge. The supremacy of faith means the supremacy of the Church».

Pobedonostsev had instilled a religious and reactionary outlook into Alexander's mind. During the period 1880-1881, Alexander blamed Grand Duke Konstantin Nikolaevich for the Constitutional project he had offered to the Tsar. Alexander condemned the idea of a representative assembly. Moreover it was Tsarevich Alexander who insisted on adopting the opposite decision establishing temporary dictatorship of a person completely devoted to the Tsar.

At first he was also against the programme of reforms Count Loris-Melikov had offered, but later he changed his mind and worked on a project of representative goverment.

After the violent death of his father, Alexander III turned the government in a reactionary direction. In his opinion, Russia was not ready for democratic reforms. Those were used by demagogues and revolutionaries in order to lead Russia into widespread social unrest. The manifesto announcing his accession affirmed autocratic power as the only one possible in Russia. It read, «We must do our best to maintain and protect the God-given autocratic power we have inherited to the benefit of our people». He stood firmly by this declared course of policy. In his reign anarchy and disturbances were temporarily stopped.

The domestic policy of Tsar Alexander III was aimed at centralization of the imperial administration. Measures were being undertaken to reduce the autonomy of rural administrations. There were some reorganizations in the economy which included the reduction of land redemptions and personal taxes, the foundation of the peasant's bank and the implementation of easy payment terms. Taking into the consideration all these steps Alexander wished to go down in history as «The Peasant Tsar».

During his years as heir apparent Alexander was a member of the State Council. He also used to attend the meetings of ministers with Tsar Alexander II.

In 1867, when there was a famine in Russia he persisted in establishing an interim Commission to distribute special aid to those suffering from starvation. It was due to the work of this Commission with Tsarevich Alexander as its President, that the aid was collected.

Alexander like his father was very good at military matters. He studied tactics under the best Russian officers. During the Russo-Turkish war of 1877-1878 he commanded the Rutshukinsky detachment. On November 14, 1877 the Russian army defeated Turkish troops near the Mechka river. It was followed by the attack of the Rutshukinsky detachment that made the Turkish army retreat. Alexander was awarded a decoration by headquarters. When he succeeded to the throne he intended to change the foreign policy of Russia. In his opinion, it had to be based on the principles of non-intervention in the sphere of interests of other countries.

In 1885 Afghanistan, inspired by Great Britain, attacked Russian detachment led by General A.V. Komarov near the Kushka river. It was completely defeated by the Russian army. So Russia faced a danger of military conflict with Great Britain. Alexander suggested convening a commission by common consent. It was due to this initiative of Alexander III that the problem was settled.

Another problem Russia felt concern about was the policy of German chancellor Bismarck aimed at the provocation of military conflicts with countries interests in the Balkans. Bismarck also planned to infringe the economic rights of Russia in Germany. The tough policy of the Tsar once again avoided a military conflict. Both diplomatic efforts undertaken by Alexander III and the concentration of Russian military forces on Western frontier made it possible to ease the tension. At the same time Russian shares, due to their low price, became greatly in demand on the Russian as well as Paris stock exchanges.

Pursuing the same course of foreign policy that met with the approval of public opinion Alexander III moved to strengthen the relationship between Russia and France. On July 1891 a French squadron led by General Jerve was invited to visit the fortress of Kronstadt and was warmly greeted there. At the same time, the arrival of Russian Admiral Avelon Toulon and Russian sailors in Paris was met with enthusiasm by French people. As a result, new peaceful tendencies were spreading far and wide in Europe. The military plots of the Austrian-German-Italian alliance were defeated. Alexander's efforts to maintain the peace in Europe won him the title «The Tsar Peacekeeper».

Although Alexander III was decidedly a man of peace he intended to improve the military position of the state. In Alexander's reign new fortresses were built and the old ones were improved. An extensive programme of railway construction was undertaken. A new type of rifle magazine and smokeless powder were introduced into the army.

Another idea Alexander III took up was the extension of military education.

Military academies were transformed into cadet corps. Military drills were preferred to classical studies. Camps were organized for cadets. Alexander attached great importance to manoeuvres and used to participate in them himself.

All these measures improved the military condition of the country. The Russian navy was also expanded. Over a short period of time Russian domination over the Black Sea area was restored. Besides that a new Baltic base and a number of shipyards were built. Ships were built by Russian craftsmen to local designs.

Alexander III emphasized that these actions were directed to the improvement of the defence of the state and had nothing in common with preparations for war.

In domestic policy, Alexander III concentrated his efforts on the consolidation of autocratic power. In this connection, he was convinced of his duty to maintain national features of Russian culture linked to Orthodoxy.

Alexander's private life was happy. On October 28, 1866 he married Princess Sophia Frederica Dagmar of Denmark, the daughter of Christian IX, King of Denmark, who had been the fiancée of his elder brother Nicholas. Her orthodox name was Maria Fyodorovna. She bore him three sons and two daughters.

Alexander III was fond of music and theatre (especially comedy). During his years as heir apparent he used to play wind instruments in a brass band.

On October 17,1888 the tsar's train coming from Sevastopol to St. Petersburg crashed near the station of Borky. Although nobody was injured it was a bitter experience for the tsar's family. It wasn't a terrorist act. Nevertheless it reminded Alexander of the terrible death of his father. The Tsar was safe but his right hip was damaged, and besides he was suffering from a pain in the small of the back, possibly the beginning of the disease he was to die of.

The last years of Alexander's reign were not favourable for the country. Indeed, they brought a turn for the worse.

In 1891 there was an attempt upon the life of the Tsarevich in Japan.

There was famine in Russia. Pobedonostsev wrote to Alexander III at the time in one of his letters, «There are many unscrupulous people trying to use the famine for their own purposes as a reason for spreading their social ideas. Leo Tolstoy has written a perverse article...»

In 1894, there was a revolt in the city of Nizhny Tagil that was suppressed with cruelty. It didn't improve the situation in the country.

Meanwhile, Alexander's health was going from bad to worse. In January 1894 the first signs of kidney disease appeared. It didn't disturb him at first but later caused the hurried departure of the Tsar's family to Livadia. But neither the climate nor the doctors could help Alexander III. He died on October 20, 1894.

Grand Duke Alexander Aleksandrovich. 1860s

*Grand Duke Alexander Aleksandrovich (centre),
his brothers Grand Dukes
Vladimir Aleksandrovich (standing) and Sergei
Aleksandrovich (right) and an unknown person.
St.Petersburg. Mid-1860s.
Photo by Levitsky.*

*Grand Duke Alexander Aleksandrovich
and his brother Vladimir Aleksandrovich.
St.Petersburg. 1860s. Photo by Levitsky.*

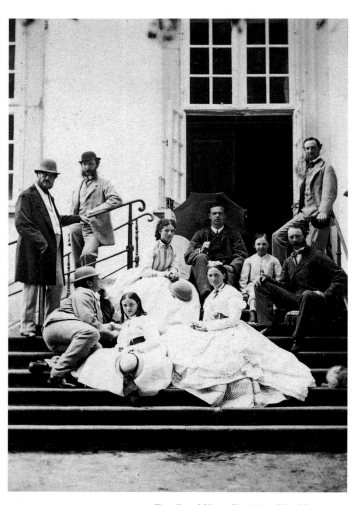

Family of King Christian IX of Denmark
with Tsarevich Alexander Aleksandrovich
and his bride Princess Dagmar.
Denmark. Mid-1860s.

Tsarevich Alexander Aleksandrovich
and his bride Princess Dagmar.
Mid-1860s.

Family of the King of Denmark with Tsarevich Alexander Aleksandrovich and Princess Dagmar. Denmark. Mid-1860s.

The lightly bluc-draped sky
Breathes bright and gentle warmth
To honour Perter's City
In September splendour.

The heavy air, warm-scented,
Brings plants their vital dew,
And the ripple of new flames
Brings harmony in peace.

Here in all these lights,
Here in this blue sky,
Is the knowledge and the style
Of a sweet and virtuous smile.

A fine day for beginnings,
As honest folk can grasp;
This the week for Dagmar
To mark the hearts of all.

Fyodor Tyutchev
Poem for the arrival in St Petersburg
of the Danish Princess Dagmar,
future Tsarina Maria Fyodorovna.

Tsarevich Alexander Aleksandrovich
and his bride Princess Dagmar.

Лeвицкій

№ 30 на Мойкѣ въ С. Петербургѣ.

*Grand Duke Alexander Aleksandrovich
(second from below),
his brother Vladimir Aleksandrovich
(third from below), and the Dukes
of Leuchtenberg. St.Petersburg. 1860s.
Photo by Levitsky.*

Лeвицкій

№ 30 на Мойкѣ въ С. Петербургѣ.

*Same. Grand Duke
Alexander Aleksandrovich
is third from the left.*

Левицкій

№ 30 на Мойкѣ въ С. Петербургѣ.

Левицкій

№ 30 на Мойкѣ въ С. Петербургѣ.

Left : Grand Duke Vladimir
Aleksandrovich and Duke Nikolai
of Leuchtenberg. St.Petersburg. 1860s.
Photo by Levitsky.

Right : Duke Nikolai
Maximilianovich of Leuchtenberg.
St.Petersburg.
Photo by Levitsky.

Grand Duke Mikhail Nikolayevich,
brother of Alexander II, hunting
in the Caucasus. Likhvano.

Tsarevich Alexander Aleksandrovich and his wife Maria Fyodorovna (centre) with their retinue, including Konstantin P. Pobedonostsev (standing right).1860s.

*Tsarevna Maria Fyodorovna.
1860s.*

*Tsarevna Maria Fyodorovna
with her children. 1870s.*

Empress Maria Fyodorovna with her son Nicholas. St. Petersburg.1880s. Photo by Levitsky.

Nicholas (right) and George,
sons of Alexander III. 1870s.

Crown Princess Maria of Greece,
Grand Duke Mikhail Aleksandrovich
and Ksenia Aleksandrovna. 1880s.

«The birth of children is the most joyful moment in
one's life, and it is impossible to describe it because
it is a very special feeling, unlike any other.»
Alexander III
From a conversation with K. Pobedonostsev

Alexander III, Maria Fyodorovna (right),
their children Ksenia and Mikhail (centre)
and entourage. Finland. 1880s.

*Left : Albert Edward, Prince of Wales.
1860s. From 1901 Edward VII,
King of Great Britain and Ireland.*

*Right : Empress Maria Fyodorovna
with her sisters. Copenhagen.*

*Alexandra, Princess of Wales,
sister of Maria Fedorovna,
the future Queen of England
with her children.*

Alexandra, Princess of Wales, with her children.

Alexander III and his retinue listening to the orchestra of the Crimean tartars. Livadia. 1886.

Alexander III with his family near a fountain in Livadia Park. 1880s.

Alexander III and Maria Fyodorovna strolling in Sebastopol. 1880s.

View of flowerbeds in Livadia Park.

«*Alexander III was truly the head of the royal family, and he kept all grand dukes and grand duchesses in their proper place: they all not only respected and honoured him, but also went in fear of him... The Emperor was convinced in mind and heart that the large imperial family, which consisted of several dozen persons of different temperaments and morality, was in duty bound to serve, in its private, public and state life, as an example to his subjects, for every awakwardness that occurs in the family of the Emperor or a Grand Duke unfailingly becomes known to the wider public and society and serves as a source of all kinds of speculations, exaggerations and legends.*»

Sergei Witte

Alexander III with his family in Livadia. The group includes Alexander III, Maria Fyodorovna, Grand Dukes Alexei and Sergei Aleksandrovich, Pavel Aleksandrovich and Elizaveta Fyodorovna. 1891.

«Most Esteemed Konstantin Petrovich,

«I have been mentally checking some of the problems which arose in the course of our recent conversation. I believe, and must repeat it once again, that there can be no doubt of the verdict of guilty for all or, at any rate, most of those indicted in connection with the train crash, both on the part of the Law Court and the Senate; and yet the hearing of the case behind closed doors would have extremely injurious moral consequences, providing new food for malicious and slanderous gossip, that would confuse the mind and heart of our gullible society. The essential circumstances of the case and the grounds for indicting persons who are directly responsible must be made public knowledge without fail...»

Anatoly Koni. From a letter to
K. Pobedonostsev in connection with
the crash of the Emperor's train
near the station of Borky
on the approaches to Kharkov.

*Alexander III, Maria Fyodorovna
and their children Nicholas, Ksenia,
George, Michael and Olga.
St.Petersburg. October 17, 1888.
Photo by Levitsky.*

«This stolid tsar (Alexander III. Ed.) did not wish ill to his empire and refused to play games with it for the simple reason that he did not understand its position and generally did not like to indulge in complex intellectual combinations that are required by a political game to no lesser degree than a game of cards. The smart lackeys of the autocratic court were quick to notice this and found it easy to persuade their credulous master that all ills stemmed from the prematurely liberal reforms of his noble-minded but over-trustful parent, that Russia was not ripe for freedom, and it was too soon to let her enter the water for she had not yet learnt to swim. Public discontent was nurtured by the incompleteness of reforms or the failure to effect them, the mere pretence of effecting them. It was decided to curtail the reforms and make no bones about it, admit it openly. The government flouted society, saying, as it were: you demanded new reforms - now the old ones will be taken away from you; you resented the dishonest misinterpretation of the reforms granted by the sovereign - well, now you are getting an honest fulfillment of the reforms misinterpreted by the sovereign.»

Vassily Klyuchevsky
«Diaries»

Above : Carriages of the tsar's train after crash. October 17, 1888.

Below : Engine and first carriages of the tsar's train after crash. October 17, 1888.

*Nicholas II and Alexandra Fyodorovna
visiting the church in Borky. 1890s.*

*Church built on the site of collision
of the tsar's train at the railway station
of Borky near Kharkov.*

Alexander III and Maria Fyodorovna
on a visit to Moscow.
Reviewing the parade. 1891.

Alexander III.1890s.

*Crowd waiting in the Kremlin
for Alexander III to step out from
the main entrance. 1891.*

*Overleaf : Alexander III and Maria
Fyodorovna arriving in Moscow in 1891.
Chudov Monastery.*

*Alexander III and Maria Fyodorovna
reviewing the ceremonial march past
of troops. 1890s.*

*Alexander III and Maria Fyodorovna
attending military exercises. 1890s.*

*Alexander III and Maria Fyodorovna
attending military exercises. 1890s.*

*Alexander III with his retinue
reviewing the ceremonial
march past of troops.
Krasnoye Selo. August 8, 1894.
Crown Prince Nikolai Aleksandrovich
on horseback.*

*Alexander III and Baron Frederick
reviewing troops on the outskirts
of Krasnoye Selo. August 8, 1894.*

Alexander III in front of the troops.
Krasnoye Selo. August 8, 1894.

*Above : Alexander III and his family
on board the Derzhava royal yacht.
August 29, 1885.*

*Alexander III with his wife and children
and officers of the Polyarnaya Zvezda
yacht at a country house in Khalila.
Early 1880s.*

*Opposite : Alexander III, Maria Fyodorovna
and their children Ksenia and George
and officers of the Polyarnaya Zvezda yacht
in Finland having a picnic. Early 1890s.*

Alexander III and Maria Fyodorovna sitting on a bench in the woods during hunting.

Arrival of Alexander III with his family for hunting in Spala in autumn. Poland. 1894.

His Imperial Highness the Grand Duke, General-Adjunct, Infantry General, Inspector-General of Schools of Higher Learning Konstantin Konstantinovich Romanov was born in Strelnya in 1858. His father was the son of Nicholas I. On reaching the age of 16 the Grand Duke became a naval cadet. Thereafter his life was closely linked with the navy. He was well known as a poet. His first publication appearing in 1882 was signed «K.R.» His book Poems of K.R. was printed four times and in 1911 the first volume of his works written in 1900-1910 saw the light of day. Apart from his poems, Konstantine Konstantinovich was known as a talented translator. He translated Shakespeare's Hamlet and Schiller's Die Braut von Messina. Both plays were staged by the translator and he acted in them.

Grand Duke Konstantin Nikolayevich with his wife Alexandra. 1860.

Grand Dukes Pavel Aleksandrovich and Konstantin Konstantinovich with their sister Olga. Venice. 1885.

Grand Duke Konstanin Konstantinovich with his wife Elizaveta and children.

*Alexander III with Maria Fyodorovna
in Denmark. Maria Fyodorovna
coming to the carriage. Copenhagen.
1880s.*

Danish prince, brother of Maria Fyodorovna,
future King Frederick VIII of Denmark.
Copenhagen.

Maria Fyodorovna, her sister
Alexandra, Princess of Wales,
and Alexander III. Copenhagen.

Children and grandchildren of King Christian IX of Denmark and queen-consort with the family of Alexander III, who married their daughter, and King George I of Greece, son of the King of Denmark. Copenhagen.

Alexander III and his family with the parents of his wife in Copenhagen.

Sojourn of Maria Fyodorovna with her children in Denmark. Seamen and officers of the Polyarnaya Zvezda yacht with members of the royal family.

Sojourn of Alexander III with his family in Denmark. Arrival in Copenhagen. The visitors are disembarking from the cutter to the pier.

Maria Fyodorovna with her children in Copenhagen. They are going to the pier from the Belle Vue Hotel.

Departure of the Russian royal family from Copenhagen.
Maria Fyodorovna with her father, the King of Denmark,
Princess of Denmark, Prince of Denmark,
and children of the Empress among others on board the
Polyarnaya Zvezda yacht.

Sojourn of Maria Fyodorovna with her children in Denmark. Seamen and officers of the Polyarnaya Zvezda yacht with members of the royal family.

*Alexander III, Maria Fyodorovna and their children
Ksenia, Olga, Michael, the Princess of Oldenburg,
the Crown Prince of Denmark
with his wife and two brothers of Maria Fyodorovna
and an unidentified person. 1890s.*

Alexander III. 1890s.

NICHOLAS II

1868 - 1918

Emperor Nicholas II and Empress Alexandra Fyodorovna with their daughters. 1901.

Russian field artillery ready for combat during the Russo-Japanese War of 1904-05.

After the accession to the Russian throne of 26-year old Nicholas II on May 14, 1896 there were expectations of changes in the domestic policy of the government. But these expectations were thwarted by the first speech of the young Emperor made after his coronation in Moscow. He said in so many words: «Let it be known that I will safeguard the principles of autocracy as firmly and steadfastly as my unforgettable late parent did.»

But it was difficult and even impossible to follow the course of Alexander III at the turn of the century. New developments were taking place on the Russian social scene, posing difficult problems for the government. The chief one was the upsurge of the revolutionary movement. By the time Nicholas II had acceded to the throne the movement of the working class in Russia was led by the revolutionary social democrats armed with the theory of Marxism which aimed at overthrowing the autocracy.

The last tsar of the Romanov dynasty had a difficult road to travel.

Even people close to the court, such as ministers Witte and Durnovo, could not unravel the character of Nicholas II because he was very reserved and good mannered. At first Witte thought he was a very «inexperienced but not dull young man with good manners». Later Witte said that the character of Nicholas II combined the traits of Paul I and Alexander I.

Nicholas II (Aleksandrovich), the eldest son of Alexander III and the Empress Maria Fyodorovna, was born at Tsarskoe Selo on May 6, 1868. He received his education from his tutor, Grigory G. Danilovich. The vast programme of general and military education was spaced over 13 years. The Emperor Alexander II demanded that emphasis should be placed on teaching Russian history and literature.

From his early years, the Tsarevich studied military service, taking part in training, reviews and parades of units which he patronized and later joining the army. In the Preobrazhensky Regiment he was a junior officer, then company commander. He also served in the cavalry life guards hussar regiment as junior officer and was promoted to squadron commander. While still a tsarevich Nicholas made a voyage to get acquainted with the navy and the construction of warships.

From 1889, Nicholas took part in the meetings of the State Council and Committee of Ministers.

In 1890, while still tsarevich, Nicholas travelled to the Far East and saw his own and other countries at first hand. His route lay via Vienna, Trieste and then by sea he visited Greece, Egypt, India, China and Japan.

The celebrations on the occasion of his arrival in Japan were spoiled by the attempt on his life made by a local nationalist. The Tsarevich was unscathed and the people of Japan resented the outrageous attack which cast a shadow over the hospitality of their country. The Tsarevich spent more than six months in foreign countries and saw the Far East and Siberia at first hand.

In Vladivostok he attended the inauguration ceremony of the construction of the Trans-Siberian Railway. He also took part in laying the foundation stone of the Vladivostok dock.

In 1892 he was appointed chairman of the committee for building the Siberian Railway.

On November 14, 1894 Nicholas married Princess Alice of Hesse-Darmstadt who was renamed Alexandra Fyodorovna. She bore him four daughters—Olga, Tatiana, Anastasia, and Maria, and the Tsarevich Alexis. In the early years of his reign Nicholas II called on all states «to put an end to continuous rearmament and find resources to prevent the misery threatening the whole world». At the Hague Conference convened at the initiative of Nicholas II on May 6, 1889 the countries of Europe, America and Asia agreed on arbitration and other methods of settling international conflicts. The Hague International Tribunal was instituted.

Inaugurating the League of Nations after World War I President Wilson of the USA asked everybody to rise to pay homage to the late Russian Emperor Nicholas II who had initiated the creation of an international organization for a peaceful settlement of differences and conflicts.

In his efforts to establish friendly relations with other countries and attaching great importance to personal contacts with the leaders of states Nicholas II made a number of trips abroad. His visit to France in October 1896 reaffirmed the alliance with that country. A trilateral agreement between Russia, France and England was reached.

The Franco-Russian alliance concluded by Nicholas II guaranteed the Western frontiers of Russia against German invasion. Russian diplomats made progress in the peaceful settlement of conflicts on the Balkan Peninsula. In 1904 Russia and Austria-Hungary signed a declaration of neutrality settling an acute conflict on the Balkan Peninsula. The Tsar's government forestalled the infiltration of Germany into the Turkish regions bordering on Russia. It succeeded in this by obtaining concessions from Turkey for building railways close to the Black Sea coast and Russo-Turkish frontier. Russia acquired a powerful influence in the Middle East.

It failed to prevent hostilities only in the Far East. At the end of the nineteenth century Japan strove to establish its predominant influence in the Pacific and Atlantic Oceans. In 1904 it attacked Russia. Without declaring war the Japanese Navy put to sea and on January 26 attacked the squadron in Port Arthur. The Japanese outnumbered the Russian armed forces. They had twice as many cruisers and three times as many destroyers as the Russian squadron in the Pacific.

A squadron of Japanese cruisers suddenly appeared at Chemulpo (Korea) in the Yellow Sea where the cruiser *Varyag* and gunboat *Koreyets* were. The Russian warships were invited to surrender. The *Varyag* accompanied by the *Koreyets* hoisted its battle flag and engaged the Japanese squadron in an unequal battle.

After losing almost all its guns and with seven officers and 115 seamen killed and wounded in this heroic battle the disabled *Varyag* and *Koreyets* retreated to the searoads in Chemulpo where the *Koreyets* was blown up and the *Varyag* sunk. The surviving members of the crew were taken to neutral ports on board foreign ships.

On February 24, 1905 Rear Admiral Makarov arrived in Port Arthur. He restored the fighting capacity of the squadron and organized the defence of Port Arthur. The Japanese fleet had to suspend military action for some time. But Makarov lost his life when his ship the *Petropavlovsk,* struck a mine. Artist Vassily Vereshchagin, the crew and staff of the admiral also died.

Hostilities on land began in April. The Japanese command besieged Port Arthur with its main forces. At the beginning of September the Japanese trenches came close to the Kumeryunsky and Vodoprovodny redoubts of the fortress.

The Japanese tightened their siege, laid mines under the fortress and used heavy 11-inch howitzers to destroy the concrete walls of the forts and batteries. Although they outnumbered the Russians three to one they could not break through the defences of Port Arthur even after a fourth assault. The fortress fell on the 157th day of the siege. Russian soldiers and sailors repeated the exploit of the defenders of Sebastopol.

The battle of Mukden, which continued for three weeks, was also lost on account of inefficient organization and lack of coordination on the part of the high command but it bled Japan white and it appealed to President

Roosevelt of the USA for his good offices in concluding a peace treaty. Nicholas II rejected this proposal.

In the middle of December the message came that Port Arthur had fallen and the whole Russian Pacific squadron had been sunk.

A squadron commanded by Vice-Admiral Zinovy Rozhestvensky engaged the Japanese fleet in the Tsushima Strait and lost the battle.

The Tsushima tragedy shocked Russia. Nicholas II agreed to conduct peace negotiations. As a result Korea found itself in the sphere of Japanese interests, the principle of the «open-door policy» was established in Manchuria and Russia ceded the southern part of Sakhalin to Japan.

The defeat of Russia in the war against Japan cost it more than 50,000 lives, the loss of the Russian fleet and adversely affected the whole life of the country.

On January 9, 1905 the Assembly of Russian Plant and Factory Workers of St.Petersburg led by priest Georgi Gapon staged a peaceful demonstration petitioning the tsar for «the truth and protection». They called for the convocation of a constituent assembly on the basis of universal, equal, direct election with a secret ballot, an eight-hour working day, equality of all estates, religious faiths, human rights, freedom of expression and strikes, amnesty for all political prisoners and cessation of the war.

Military force was used against the unarmed workers. On the day after the tragic events Nicholas II said, speaking to St.Petersburg Governor-General Dmitry F. Trepov, that it was extremely necessary now in addition to strict measures to show the government's fairness and concern for the good and peaceable majority of the working people.

But it was too late to halt growing discontent. In October strikes spread to the central cities of Russia.

Nicholas II agreed to create conditions for universal suffrage. On October 17 the Tsar signed the manifesto expressing the «unswerving Royal's will» to grant civil liberties on the basis of the inviolability of the person, freedom of conscience, expression, assembly and trades unions and to convene a legislative State Duma.

The promulgation of the Tsar's manifesto and convocation of the State Duma set in motion the activity of various parties representing every segments of society.

After the institution of the State Duma in the period of the revolutionary movement of 1905-07 Nicholas II began to support and promote the agrarian legislation drafted by the minister of the interior, Pyotr R. Stolypin. The Tsar's decree to the Senate of November 9, 1906 was the first step towards the abolition of communal land use in Russia. Peasant ownership of land was recognized. The third Duma approved the decree and on June 14, 1910 it became law. Stolypin's land reform encouraged efficient development of the private peasant economy along the lines of market production. During the reign of Nicholas II, in addition to the large-scale land reform, some other important economic and social measures were taken. On June 7, 1899 the monetary statute was adopted. Its implementation served to increase money resources. Conversion to gold-backed money circulation increased gold reserves, peasants' banks were established, small credit and land improvement credit institutions were created. Local courts were reformed and exile was abolished. Measures of protection of trade and industry were taken. Construction of railways and roads was stepped up.

By 1908 the economic situation in Russia had stabilized and the country was on the way to economic growth. The living standards of the population improved, as was evidenced by the growth of savings, the state budget, grain yields, industry and trade, including foreign trade.

On the eve of World War I the international situation in Western Europe grew extremely tense.

The British Ambassador to Russia George Buchanan wrote that Nicholas II exercised all his influence in favour of peace. He was ready to make any concessions to prevent the horrors of war. At the end of 1913 there was the impression that Russia would never enter the war. Unfortunately, this impression provoked Germany to take advantage of the situation.

On December 23, 1913 foreign minister Sazonov reported to Nicholas II that the growing claims of Germany and its allies could be transferred to the Western frontier and that it was impossible to be reconciled with this situation. «I can see clearly that we will not be able to keep peace for long », said the Emperor. The programmes of the country's rearmament in view of the impending threat from Germany were designed for three or four years, that is, they could be completed by 1917. Germany was already prepared for war and was looking for a pretext to start a conflict and carry out its predatory plans for a redivision of the world.

The German minister for foreign affairs reported in the summer of 1914: «Today Russia is not prepared for war...According to competent estimates, in a few years Russia will re-establish its fighting capacity. Then it will overwhelm us with the great numbers of its soldiers, its Baltic fleet will be built and its strategic railways will be constructed.»

On June 15, 1914 a Serbian nationalist assassinated Franz Ferdinand, heir to the Austrian throne, in Sarajevo (Bosnia).

Austria declared war on Serbia, on July 19 Germany declared war on Russia and on July 21 on France and on July 22 England declared war on Germany. The war in Europe grew into a world war.

From the very beginning of military operations the allies brought pressure to bear on Russia to make her change her plan of general operations. The victorious offensive of German troops in Western Europe and their fast advance to Paris threatened France with defeat. Throughout the war Nicholas II remained faithful to his obligations to the allies. To give assistance to the French army as soon as they could the First and Second Russian armies had to invade Eastern Prussia before they had concentrated their forces and were combat ready. To beat off the Russian offensive the Germans sent two infantry corps and a cavalry division at a time when the situation in France was critical. The Germans lost their battle in France because their forces on the Western front were impaired. The Russian army paid a high price for coming to the rescue of its allies. It lost 150,000 men in the fighting.

At that time a major battle was fought in the south-western area which was most important for Russia. Russia had many important victories to its credit. Its army advanced 280-300 kilometres capturing Galicia and its capital Lvov. Germany's hopes for a swift war were dashed and its conclusion was postponed «for an indefinite time».

Regrouping their forces on the vast front the Russians stood up to the advancing German army on both banks of the Vistula. By the end of October 1914 the German army had been driven back to its former positions. The Russians scored their victories when the Germans advanced on Flanders. Once again the German command had to stop their offensive in France to repulse the Russian offensive.

The Russian front became the main theatre of military operations. The German high command had to change the whole plan of war.

The course of the war with Russia tempted Germany to conclude a separate peace with her. The peace terms offered by Germany were favourable for Russia but Nicholas II refused to conduct negotiations and honoured his obligations under the treaty with the Entente powers because he thought Russia's withdrawal from the war would be a treacherous act.

Turkey's entry into the war on the side of Germany created a new front in Transcaucasia and on the Black Sea. The situation deteriorated even further in the autumn of 1915 when Bulgaria joined the German block.

Russia held back the offensive of 134 German divisions and more than half the Turkish army.

The successful German offensive in 1915 was mainly due to the fact that the Russian army was short of artillery, rifles and amunition and received no assistance from its allies. Putting up stubborn resistance the Russian army retreated from Galicia, Poland, part of the Baltic states and Belorussia.

On May 22, 1916 Russian troops launched an offensive against fortified enemy positions on the south-western front. General Brusilov commanded four armies participating in the offensive. He employed a new tactic of breaking through enemy defences by attacking from different directions at the same time with the support of a heavy artillery barrage. This operation won admiration throughout the world and was later known as «the Brusilov break-through». When Russian troops suffered a series of setbacks in August 1915 Nicholas II assumed the post of Supreme Commander in Chief instead of the Grand Duke Nikolai Nikolayevich. The Tsar believed in victory and thought that the retreat was temporary and that the shortage of arms would be overcome. Appearing in front of the soldiers together with his son Tsarevich Alexis Nicholas sought to strengthen patriotic feeling.

But ominous developments were gaining momentum in the country. The war called for strenuous economic efforts, the food problem grew acute. The ties with the world market to which Russia supplied a lot of grain, flax, hemp, butter and other products, had been ruptured.

The war put Russia to a severe test. Continuation of hostilities and setbacks at the front imposed a heavy burden on the economy.

The leader of the Constitutional Democrats, N. Milyukov, appealed to the country to put aside internal disagreements and fulfil the sacred duty of every Russian citizen: «To keep the country united and indivisible and hold its position among the world powers which is challenged by the enemy.»

The Labour Peasant Party called for «defending the Russian land and culture against the German invasion» and putting off the problems of «dealing with internal reactionaries» until after the war.

The Bolshevik Party took a different stand. Its programme on war, peace and revolution included the provision for Russia's defeat in the war. Lenin put forward the slogan of turning the imperialist war into a civil one and of transforming the imminent bourgeois democratic revolution in Russia into a socialist one. Lenin emphasised that the proletariat should not defend its Motherland in the world war but should work for the defeat of its government.

The economic, philosophical, historical and diplomatic arguments in favour of the need to defend the country against the German invasion put forward by Social Revolutionaries and Mensheviks, including Georgi V. Plekhanov, who called on everyone «to put all efforts, heart and feeling» into the struggle of Russia against Prussian junkers, came under sharp criticism in all publications of the Bolshevik Party. In August 1915 Lenin formulated his plan for a possible proletarian revolution in one country alone. The enormous loss of human lives and shortage of food created favourable conditions for revolutionary agitation.

The Russian monarch did not appreciate the danger threatening the country in the extremely difficult and complicated war situation. Preoccupied with the war he did not doubt its successful outcome for Russia in the near future. In his reminiscences, German General Erich Ludendorff wrote about the difficult situation of German troops in 1917: «Our situation is extremely difficult and it is almost impossible to find a solution. If the war goes on our defeat seems to be inevitable».

By 1917 Russia had brought its military potential to the level needed to ensure its superiority over the enemy. Winston Churchill assessed the situation in Russia on the eve of the February Revolution as stable and thought that after all the sacrifices in the war victory seemed to be certain. The Tsar regarded rallies, demonstrations and strikes as consequences of the food crisis. When revolutionary unrest and demonstrations flared up in St.Petersburg in the beginning of February 1917 it was decided to deliver 48 tons of bread to the capital. The tsar was informed that the danger of the revolution had been warded off. On February 21 the Tsar left St.Petersburg for his high command headquarters. The emergency measures on which the Grand Duke Mikhail insisted were not introduced in the capital.

On the morning of February 28 the trains of Nicholas II with travel warrants left Moghilev for Tsarskoe Selo but were halted at the Troshino Station. Nicholas II had to go to Pskov, headquarters of the Northern Front. Rodzyanko cabled the Tsar that he had to abdicate from the throne or the Duma would be divested of power. On the night of March 3 the Tsar signed the abdication document in his railway car.

On March 22 Nicholas was taken to Tsarskoe Selo where his family resided. They lived in total seclusion. In his efforts to discover that the Tsar and his consort were guilty of treason the chairman of the Provisional Government, Kerensky, made ten visits to Tsarskoe Selo and perused the Tsar's confiscated papers.

The Provisional Government set up an extraordinary commission to investigate «the case of treason» of the Tsar's family headed by Mikhail K. Muraviev. They did not find anything that might compromise the reputation of the Tsar and his consort, but the investigation findings were not made public.

Once he had been arrested the fate of the Tsar was sealed. He was doomed to die. In his reminiscences Vladimir D. Nabokov, chief of the administrative department of the Provisional Government, wrote that the arrest of the Tsar «tied a knot which was cut in Yekaterinburg».

In his darkest days all the people close to the Emperor, whom he trusted for their loyalty and friendship, abandoned him and fled. In his diary Nicholas II wrote: «Treachery, cowardice and deception on all sides».

When the question of the departure of the Royal family from Russia was raised Nicholas II agreed to go to England. On March 23 George V, King of England, agreed to give refuge to the deposed Russian monarch. But the Provisional Government delayed its answer. Weeks passed by and after the expiry of one month the British king, cousin and friend of Nicholas II, related in kinship with his consort, cancelled his agreement with the Provisional Government under the influence of his prime minister David Lloyd George.

Soon after the October Revolution all the members of House of Romanov on the territory of Russia were arrested and murdered. The Grand Duke Mikhail Aleksandrovich was the first of the royal family to die.

*Left : Tsarevich
Nikolai Aleksandrovich. 1890s.*

*Right : Princess Alice of Hesse
(later renamed Alexandra
Fyodorovna) with her brother Ernst-
Ludwig,
the Crown Prince of Hesse.
Early 1890s.*

*Grand Duke Georgi Aleksandrovich,
Grand Duchess Ksenia Aleksandrovna
and Tsarevich Nikolai Aleksandrovich
on the royal yacht. 1880s.*

Emperor Nicholas II with his wife
Alexandra Fyodorovna.
Grand Duchess Maria Pavlovna
(elder), wife of Grand Duke Vladimir
Aleksandrovich, is on the right,
Grand Duke Sergei Mikhailovich
is standing in the centre,
the others are unidentified. Mid-1890s.

Tsarevich Nikolai Aleksandrovich among the envoys of the Don Cossacks. 1890s.

Tsarevich Nikolai Aleksandrovich and
Alice of Hesse (standing left).
Right to left: Grand Duke Sergei
Aleksandrovich, Ernst-Ludwig of
Hesse, Victoria of Saxe-Coburg-Gotha,
Grand Duchess Elizaveta Fyodorovna,
Victoria of Battenberg, and Irene
of Prussia. Darmstadt. 1894.

Left to right: Grand Duke Ernst-Ludwig of Hesse, brother of Aleksandra Fyodorovna, Empress Aleksandra Fyodorovna, Emperor Nicholas II, Princess Irene of Prussia, her husband Henry of Prussia, Grand Duchess Elizaveta Fyodorovna, Grand Duke Sergei Aleksandrovich, Princess Victoria of Battenberg and her husband Prince Ludwig of Battenberg. Early 1900s.

Opposite: Empress Maria Fyodorovna and Tsarevich Nikolai Aleksandrovich in Copenhagen. Standing behind the chair is Queen Louisa of Denmark, mother of Maria Fyodorovna, and Prince George, later George V, King of Great Britain. Sitting in the background is Princess Alexandra of Wales, sister of Maria Fyodorovna. Early 1890s.

Aleksandra Fyodorovna.
1890s

Nicholas II, Aleksandra Fyodorovna and Elizaveta Fyodorovna. 1890s.

*Above : Moscow during the coronation
of Nicholas II. 1896.*

*Below : Corpses of people who died
in the crush Khodynka Field during the
coronation. Moscow. 1896.*

*Opposite : Identification of bodies
picked up on Khodynka Field.
Moscow. 1896.*

Right : Empress Aleksandra Fyodorovna. 1907.

Emperor Nicholas II.

The Emperor and his consort
visiting the Trinity-St.Sergius Laura.
August 18, 1898.

*The Emperor and his consort
in the Trinity-St.Sergius Laura. 1898.*

*Departure of the Tsar
and his consort from the Sergiyevo
railway station. 1898.*

Left to right: Grand Dukes Andrei Vladimirovich, Pyotr Nikolayevich, Pavel Aleksandrovich and Vladimir Aleksandrovich, Aleksandra Fyodorovna, Yelena Vladimirovna, Maria Pavlovna, Nicholas II, Pyotr Aleksandrovich, Prince of Oldenburg, Grand Dukes Konstantin Konstantinovich, Sergei Mikhailovich, Dmitry Konstantinovich, an unidentified person and the Duke of Mecklenburg. Strelnya. 1899.

*Nicholas II
with his daughter Olga. 1895.*

*Nicholas II
and Aleksandra Fyodorovna. 1895.*

Nicholas II and Aleksandra Fyodorovna with members of the royal family, seamen and officers

*Aleksandra Fyodorovna
with daughters Maria,
Olga and Tatiana. 1899.*

*Tsarevich Nikolai Aleksandrovich
with his bride Alice of Hesse.
Coburg. 1894.*

«*There is something wonderful in the love of
two souls who have merged into one, who hide
not a single thought from each other; they share
joy and suffering, well-being and need, and
from the first kiss till the last breath sing to
each other of love alone.*»
Empress Aleksandra Fyodorovna
A notation in the diary of her fiancé the
Grand Duke Nikolai Aleksandrovich

*Nicholas II and Aleksandra Fyodorovna
with daughters
Olga and Tatiana. 1897.*

*Aleksandra Fyodorovna
with her
daughter Olga. 1895.*

Tsarevich Alexei Nikolayevich.
Tsarskoe Selo. 1907.

Daughters of Nicholas II: Olga,
Tatiana, Maria, and Anastasia. 1904.

*Aleksandra Fyodorovna
with her daughters. 1900s.*

*Nicholas II with his daughters,
Doctor Botkin and others
on his visit to Germany. 1910s.*

*Nicholas II and Aleksandra Fyodorovna
with their daughters and son, relatives
of Aleksandra Fyodorovna and people
close to them. Darmstadt. 1910.*

Above and following pages :
Nicholas II attending large-scale
military exercises near Kursk. 1902.

Nicholas II leaving the
Red Cross infirmary. Kursk. 1902.

Members of the Kursk administration
are introduced to Nicholas II outside
the infirmary
of the reserve battalion.

*Nicholas II
visiting a military unit.*

*Nicholas II with the officers
of the unit he visited.*

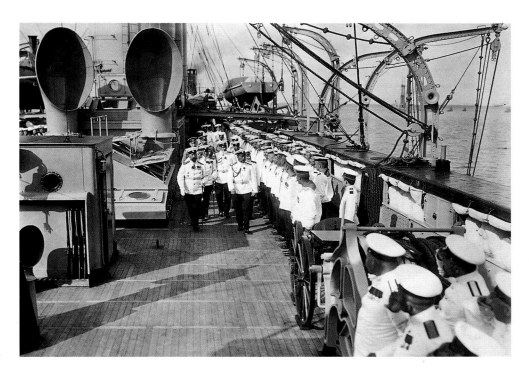

Nicholas II in a naval unit.

Nicholas II visiting Hospital No.16 of the Russian Zemstvo Union.

Overleaf: A group of uhlans of Her Majesty with Nicholas II, Aleksandra Fyodorovna and their daughters Olga and Tatiana attending military exercises in Krasnoye Selo. 1908.

Left: Tsarevich Aleksei Nikolayevich. 1907.

Right : Tsarevich Aleksei Nikolayevich. 1908.

Left: Nicholas II with his sister Grand Duchess Olga Aleksandrovna on board the royal yacht.

Opposite: Nicholas II and Tsarevich Aleksei Nikolayevich. 1910s.

Nicholas II attending military exercises in Krasnoye Selo.

169

Nicholas II and Aleksandra Fyodorovna
*wearing the costumes of the Tsar
Aleksei Mikhailovich and Tsarina
Maria Ilyinichna. St. Petersburg. 1903*

*Bicentennial of the foundation
of St. Petersburg. 1903*

*Opposite: Bicentennial of the
foundation of St.Petersburg. 1903.*

*Public prayer on the bicentennial
of the foundation of St.Petersburg. 1903.*

The Grand Duchess Elizaveta Fyodorovna, the elder sister of the Empress, was married to the Grand Duke Sergei Aleksandrovich. After his death she became Mother Superior of the St.Martha and St Maria Convent.

In 1917 she was arrested and sent together with the nuns Varvara and Ekaterina, first to Ekaterinburg and then to Alapayevsk, Perm Province, 140 kilometres north of Ekaterinburg. On July 18, 1918 after cruel beating she was thrown into a pit with the other detainees and buried alive. The investigation established that when she was about to die the Grand Duchess Elizaveta Fyodorovna managed to bandage in the pit the head of the Prince Johann Konstantinovich who was dying next to her. Recently Elizaveta Fyodorovna was canonized a saint of the Russian Orthodox Church.

Grand Duchess
Elizaveta Fyodorovna.

Opposite:
Grand Duke Sergei Aleksandrovich
Grand Duchess Elizaveta Fyodorovna

Grand Duchess Elizaveta Fyodorovna.
Same. 1880s.

Prince Henry of Prussia with
his wife Irene (sister of Aleksandra
Fyodorovna) and son Wilhelm.

The Grand Duke Sergei Aleksandrovich Romanov, the fourth son of the Emperor Alexander II, was born on April 29, 1857.
In 1881 the Grand Duke made a journey across Europe and to Palestine. Following his trip to the holy places an Orthodox Palestinian Society was formed under the chairmanship of His Highness. Its aim was to gather, prepare and disseminate in Russia information about the holy places in the Orient and assist pilgrims. At the suggestion of His Highness the Society made successful excavations in Jerusalem with the money he had donated.
From 1891 the Grand Duke was Moscow Governor-General. He was assassinated by the terrorist Kalyayev.

Grand Duke Sergei Aleksandrovich with his wife Elizaveta Fedorovna.

177

*Their Majesties approaching
the Iberian chapel of the Holy Virgin.*

*Nicholas II and Aleksandra
Fyodorovna visiting Moscow in 1903.*

Nicholas II in Moscow. 1903.

Opposite: Nicholas II and Aleksandra Fyodorovna in Moscow. 1903.

Nicholas II and Aleksandra Fyodorovna being welcomed in the Kremlin. Moscow. 1903

*Opposite: The Japanese setting off
a mine under the parapet of Fort 2
before the assault. 1904.*

*Reviewing the crews of
the Varyag and Koreyets cruisers
in front of the Winter Palace.*

*Opposite: Cossack regiment
on its way to a meeting with the sailors of the Varyag and Koreyets cruisers. Fontanka embankment.
St Petersburg. 1904.*

*Nicholas II reviewing the crews
of the Varyag and Koreyets cruisers
on the Palace Square.
St.Petersburg. 1904.*

*Hospital train leaving for the front.
Russo-Japanese War*

«*The new year of 1904 began fortissimo - with the thunder of the sudden war against Japan. This came as something quite unexpected for us, for all the people of our circle. But it appeared that other circles, those who should have been in the know, were not quite prepared either. This was the first real war Russia was drawn into since 1878, but in the beginning nobody took it seriously and almost all treated it with amazing recklessness - as a trifling adventure, from which Russia could not but emerge victorious...*

«*However, Russian society did not remain ignorant of the true strength of the new and despised enemy for long...*»

Alexander Benua

The Tsar reviewing the troops leaving for Russia's Far East. The crews of the Varyag and Koreyets in front of the Winter Palace. 1904.

188

Building field fortifications.
Russo-Japanese War. 1904.

«Why was the Emperor Nicholas II destined to rule at the beginning of the 20th century, during one of the most troubled periods known to history? A man of integrity, the embodiment of all that is most noble and chivalrous in Russian nature, he lacked strength... He despised the wiles of diplomacy and was not fitted for struggle; events brought him to ruin.

«Nicholas II was modest and shy. He was too unsure of himself: hence all his failures. More often than not, his first impulse was right, but his ill fortune consisted in that, distrusting hiself, he rarely followed it. He sought advice from people he regarded as more knowledgeable than himself, and from that moment ceased to be master of the situation: it slipped out of his hands; he vacillated between opposite opinions and often ended by siding with the one that went most contrary to his own feeling.»

Pierre Gilliard
«Emperor Nicholas II and His Family»

Fire at the foot of Zolotaya Hill.
Port Arthur. 1904

Nicholas II with the icon of St.Serafim Sarovsky bidding farewell to an infantry regiment before it is sent to the front. Peterhof. 1905.

Overleaf: Nicholas II reviewing the troops leaving for the front during the Russo-Japanese War. 1904.

Building fortifications in the environs of Port Arthur. 1904.

Russo-Japanese War.
After an attack. 1904.

The Japanese building trenches
during the Russo-Japanese War. 1904.

*Vice-Admiral
Stepan Ossipovitch Makarov.*

*Opposite: Mass grave
of the fallen in the Russo-Japanese
War of 1904-05. Port Arthur.
Photo taken in 1945.*

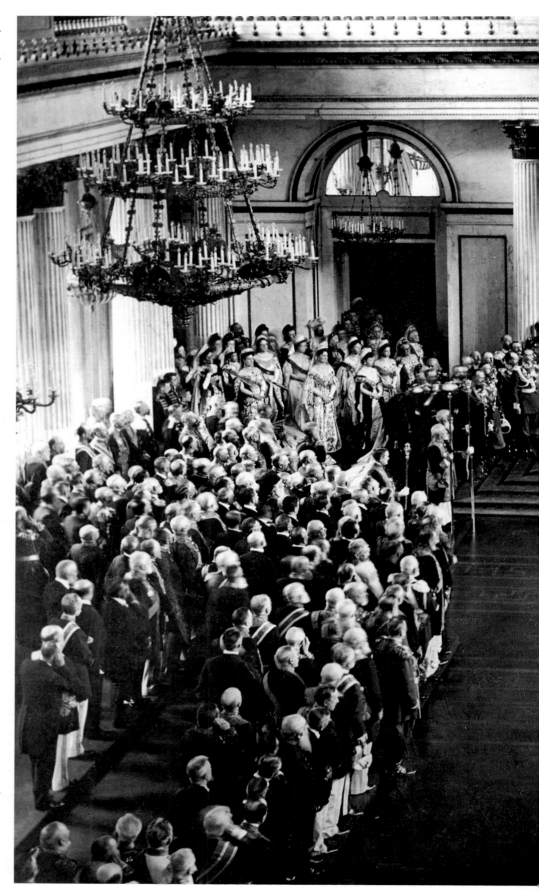

Nicholas II's speech on the opening of the State Duma and State Council in the Winter Palace. April 27, 1906.

Nicholas II reviewing the troops on parade. Tsarskoe Selo. 1906.

After unveiling the monument.
Kiev. 1911.

Nicholas II in Kiev. Public prayer
at the monument to Alexander II
on the day of its unveiling. 1911.

Sojourn of the royal family in Moscow.
August 1912.

Public prayer in Red Square.

*Emperor Nicholas II with his consort
and family in Red Square.
Moscow. 1912.*

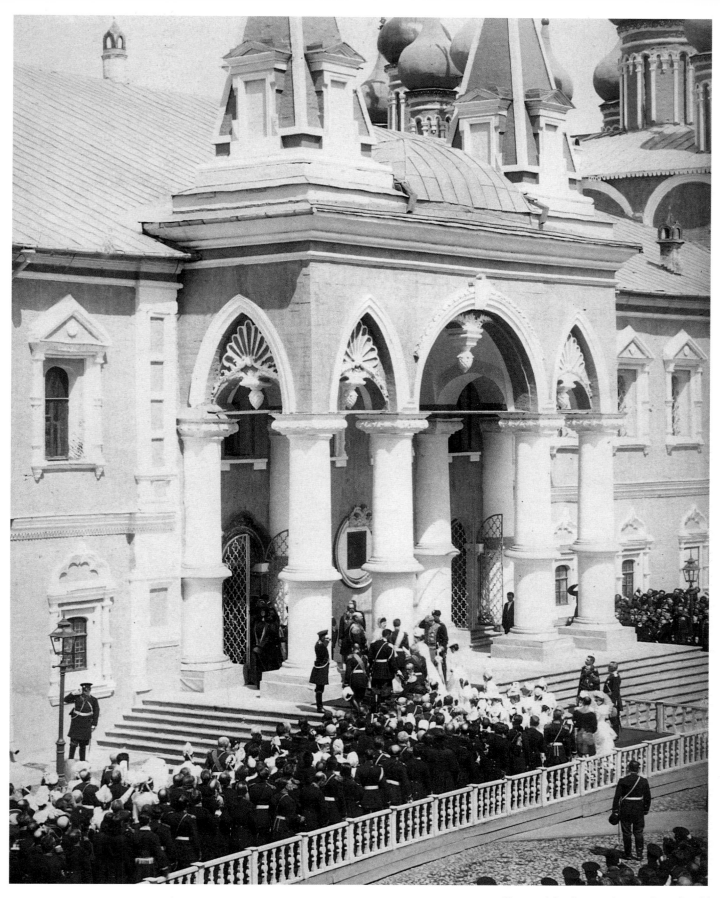

*The royal family stepping out from the old
Romanov Palace in the Kremlin accompanied
by their retinue and courtiers. Moscow. 1912.*

Nicholas II inspecting the officers' formation on the platform. August 1912.

Nicholas II on the railway platform in Moscow. August 1912

Nicholas II and Aleskandra Fyodorovna
with the Crown Prince Alexis
in the carriage at the entrance to the Tsar's
rooms at the railway station.

Religious procession in the Kremlin.
August 1912.

Nicholas II passing by a formation of schoolboys. Moscow. 1912.

*Nicholas II passing by schoolgirls
standing by the Ivan the Great
Bell-Tower. Moscow. 1912.*

Nicholas II in the Kremlin. Moscow.
August 1912.

Nicholas II with his wife and son.
Baron Frederick in the background.
Moscow. August 1912.

Opposite: Palace Grenadiers marching
past the monument to Alexander III.
Moscow. August 1912.

Overleaf: In front of the
Cathedral of Christ the Saviour.
Moscow. August 1912.

Emperor Nicholas II.

At the monument to Alexander II.
Moscow. 1912.

Passage of the Tsar's carriage by
the Arc de Triomphe.
Moscow. August 1912

*Nicholas II with his daughters
at the monument to Alexander II
in the Kremlin. Moscow. August 1912.*

Nicholas II and Maria Fyodorovna at the Cathedral of Christ the Saviour. Moscow. August 1912.

Opposite: Palace Grenadiers in front of the Cathedral of Christ the Saviour. Moscow. 1912.

*Above: Nicholas II with his mother
the Dowager Empress Maria
Fyodorovna visiting the Alexander III
Museum on Volkhonka. Moscow. 1912.*

*Below : Nicholas II departing from
the Alexander III Museum.*

*Nicholas II with his mother
and daughters leaving the Alexander
III Museum. Moscow. 1912.*

On May 15, 1913 Nicholas II with his family
and retinue left Tsarskoe Selo for the 300th
anniversary celebrations of the Romanov
dynasty. The route of the royal train lay via
Vladimir, Suzdal, Nizhny Novgorod,
Kostroma, Yaroslavl, Rostov Veliky, Pereslavl
and Moscow.

300th anniversary of the Romanov
House. Nicholas II arriving
in Kostroma with his retinue. 1913.

*Empress Aleksandra Fyodorovna
with her sister Elizaveta Fyodorovna
in Kostroma. 1913.*

*300th anniversary of the Romanov
dynasty. Nicholas II in Kostroma.
The Tsarevich Alexis ship. 1913.*

On visiting Kostroma and St.Hipatius Monastery which went down in history as the cradle of the Romanov dynasty Nicholas II paid homage to the ancient cathedrals and the miracle-working icon of St.Theodore and took part in laying the foundation stone of a monument and in a military parade.

Nicholas II and Aleksandra Fyodorovna in Kostroma. 1913.

Nicholas II and Aleksandra Fyodorovna in the church in Kostroma. 1913.

The royal family went to see the Romanov Museum in Kostroma with its rich and rare collection. The local gentry donated a generous sum of 500,000 roubles for educational purposes. The illumination of the city was especially impressive owing to the recent installation of electric lighting.

The Emperor and the Empress leaving the Romanov Museum in Kostroma. 1913.

His misfortune was to be born an autocrat despite being temperamentally unsuited to this role. In truth, he never governed Russia, and because he allowed the ruling aristocracy to disregard the pledges of liberty of speech, of assembly, etc..., contained in his 1905 manifesto, the people largely withdrew their trust from him. The dynastic burden weighed increasingly heavily on him as his reign proceeded; this was a vast empire with an almost 75 per cent illiteracy rate, where the revolutionary spirit of 1905 had never died, where the revolutionary spirit of 1905 had never died, where the Church - with had become a state department like any other since Peter the Great's abolition of the Patriarchate - was rapidly losing its attraction for ordinary people, as a result of the scandalous appointments made under Rasputin's direct influence; where Justice was corrupt and almost every branch of administration lay in the hands of men who were either incompetent or thoroughly dubious; and to all this what should be added but the World War ! The whole system collapsed and the wretched Tsar was certainly not the man to put it back together again.

Georges Buchaman

300th anniversary of the Romanov dynasty. Nicholas II with his family arriving in Sergiyevo.

300th anniversary of the Romanov dynasty. People waiting for the arrival of the royal family in Moscow. 1913.

Nicholas II at Novospassky Monastery. 1913.

Nicholas II in Tsarskoe Selo. 1910s.

Nicholas II in Bobruisk.
World War I, 1914.

Emperor seeing off military units
leaving for the front.

Opposite, above : Nicholas II
in Peremysl. 1914.

Opposite, below : Nicholas II
inspecting the battlefront.
Peremysl. 1914.

Nicholas II at railway station
in Baranovichi. 1914.

Gun pieces in battle positions.
World War I.

Above opposite:
At the front. World War I.

Opposite:
Nicholas II and Commander-in-Chief
Grand Duke Nikolai Nikolayeveich
(Junior) in theatre of military opera-
tions. World War I.

243

*Nicholas II, royal court minister Iudelov,
Adjutant-General Count Vladimir
B.Fredericks and Palace Commandant
Major-General V.Voyeikov. Baranovichi.
Headquarters of the Supreme
Commander-in-Chief. World War I.*

Nicholas II in area of military hostilities.
World War I.

Nicholas II and Grand Duke Nikolai
Nikolayevich (Junior) visiting military
units in Belorussia. World War I.

Opposite: World War I.
Glimpses of life of the
Eighth Army.
Soldiers marching past
the Emperor General Kornilov.

Nicholas II in headquarters of
Supreme Command. Standing
at his side is Tsarevich Alexis.

Nicholas II leaving makeshift
church in Baranovichi.

Opposite:
General Kornilov at the front.

Opposite, above:
Nicholas II inspecting battleground.

Opposite, below:
World War I.
Nicholas II inspecting damage
after battle.

Soldiers and officers greeting
Emperor in theatre of military operations.
World War I.

Grigori Rasputin
among his admirers.

Grigori Rasputin was born in Pokrovskoye
Village, Tyumen District, Tobolsk Province in
1863 into the family of a peasant and fisher-
man, Yefim Vasilyevich. He was married to a
peasant woman and had three children.
In St.Petersburg Grigori Rasputin was presented
at the court.
S.P.Beletsky, one of the courtiers, who was well
acquainted with Rasputin's relationship with the
royal family, wrote: «He was admitted to the
palace with the support of various persons, including the late Count Sergei Witte and Prince
Meshchersky. The latter put his hopes in him as
a vehicle of influence in high circles. Rasputin
saw the mystically-minded nature of the
Emperor...assessed the slightest turns of his mind
and will, instilled the faith in his (Rasputin's)
foresight by foretelling the appearance of the heir
and strengthened this faith by taking advantage
of the disease of the Tsarevich Alexis, increased
his influence on the Emperor by suggesting that he
(Rasputin) alone possessed the mysterious powers
to treat the disease of the heir and maintain the
life of His Highness and that Rasputin was sent
by Providence for «the well-being and happiness
of the august family».

Grigori Rasputin, Bishop Germogen
and monk Iliodor.
(S.N.Trufanov in the world).

Grigori Rasputin with his children.

Grigori Rasputin.

Nicholas II in front of the Cathedral
of Christ the Saviour.
Fragment of photo. 1912.

*Nicholas II during his detention
after abdication from the throne.
Tsarskoe Selo. 1917.*